MW00768303

From
Seeker
To
Finder

Discovering Everyday Happiness

GEORGE KIMELDORF, Ph. D.

From Seeker to Finder: Discovering Everyday Happiness
Copyright 2013 by George Kimeldorf.

All rights reserved. No part of this book may be reproduced in any form or by any electronic or mechanical means without written permission of the publisher, except by a reviewer, who may quote brief passages in a review.

Published by Newlog Publishing Company
an imprint associated with YYP Group, Ltd.
info@yypgroup.com

Newlog Publishing Company
15707 Coit Rd., Suite C-114
Dallas, TX 75248-4463

Library of Congress Control Number 2012923440

ISBN 978-0-9887602-0-2

To my happiness teachers: Susan Gregg, Gary van Warmerdam, Don Miguel Ruiz, and especially Barbara Emrys

ACKNOWLEDGMENTS

This book arose as an expression of gratitude, generosity, and love by numerous people. My wife Carol encouraged me throughout the project, reviewed drafts of each chapter, and proposed many improvements to the text. My first student, Jude Fox, also made many helpful editorial suggestions, especially regarding phrasing and transitions between topics. Although the material was mine, Jude's collaboration on the first draft almost amounted to co-authorship. Many others also read parts of the manuscript at various states and gave valuable suggestions. In particular, my thanks to Robyn Jamison, who meticulously line-edited a previous draft, and to Jim Morris for his encouragement after reading the final manuscript.

TABLE OF CONTENTS

CHAPTER 1

Finding Happiness

I've been alive 25,567 days. That is a long time. All I have ever wanted during that time was to be happy—nothing more.

I thought I knew what I needed to do to be happy, so I did all those things: I earned a Ph. D. in mathematics, married a wonderful woman, raised two lovely children, pursued a successful career as a mathematics professor, and became wealthy. Everything seemed fine. But the joy, satisfaction, and peace of mind I so desired continued to elude me.

At age 35, I began to realize that the "right" things would not get me what I wanted, so I actively sought happiness by doing workshops, reading self-help books, leading seminars, practicing self-hypnosis, and meditating. I became a seeker.

Only in the past few years did real transformation begin. I am no longer a seeker; I am a finder. Despite doubting in the past that I would ever succeed, I have found the happiness and peace of mind I had long sought.

I actually love life.

I love the world, and I especially love and accept myself. I have discovered that we can really love the world and all the people in it, despite the violence, hatred, crime, hypocrisy, greed, suffering, and starvation.

I am celebrating my 70th birthday as I write the first pages of this book. During this 70-year journey, I have discovered many things. To my utter amazement, I found that learning to be happy is not mystical, mysterious, or magical[1]. Happiness is an ordinary skill that anybody can learn and master through practice, like driving a car or playing a violin. And like driving a car or playing the violin, happiness is an experiential skill which cannot be learned from reading books.

If happiness cannot be taught in a book, why am I writing this? The first purpose of this book is to tell you what does not work. In my quest for happiness, I pursued many fruitless paths. What if I had achieved happiness earlier in life, rather than having spent decades following roads leading nowhere? Had I read a book such as this, I might have avoided some of these pitfalls and shortened some of these detours. By

---

[1] Other than sex, I enjoy nothing more than alliteration.

sharing my experience, I hope to spare you years of looking in the wrong places.

Most people spend their entire lifetimes seeking happiness in places where, at best, it is only temporarily experienced. Their parents, teachers, and religious leaders falsely promised them as children that hard work, financial success, acquisition of goods, and approval from others will make them happy. Our culture spreads these illusory expectations through movies, books, TV, and advertising. When people achieve these goals hoping to be happy and then realize that they are not in fact happy, their unfulfilled expectations lead to disappointment, dissatisfaction, disillusionment, and discouragement.[2] To make matters worse, they often blame themselves for this perceived failure, leading to feelings of powerlessness and despair.

Other people, having read books or attended seminars, are seekers. They know that they cannot achieve happiness through financial success, acquisition of goods, or approval of others. They know that happiness results from experiencing gratitude, acceptance, self-love, and forgiveness. They have learned that the path to happiness is through awareness of their thoughts, doubting their beliefs, changing their points of view, and expressing unconditional love. Yet they remain seekers. Although they know what to do to become happy, the true joy,

---

[2] I told you. I love alliteration.

peace of mind, satisfaction, and contentment which they fervently seek continues to elude them.

I have met dozens of such seekers, who are unwittingly driving with their left foot on the brake pedal. Until they discover and confront how they are holding themselves back, they will forever remain seekers. In later chapters, I will describe my good fortune in finding teachers who not only made me aware of how I was pressing that pedal, but also assured me that it was safe to release my foot from the brake.

The second reason for writing this book is to tell you about the path by which I have achieved my current state of happiness, joy, and peace of mind. Perhaps it will inspire you to pursue a similar goal. Will my path work for you? I do not know. I know that it has worked for me, as well as for many other people. I also know others who, after learning about this path, have decided not to pursue it. I respect their decision. It is not for everybody.

When you watch young children, have you noticed their obvious excitement in being alive, their natural curiosity, their joy, their spontaneity? Two minutes after being hurt, they are laughing and ready to play. We were all once young children. What happened to our spark, spirit, and spunk?[3] Can this joy of life be revived? Why do so many of us instead experience cynicism, resignation, and discontent? Must we take life so seriously? As you read, I encourage you

---

[3] I won't disturb you by footnoting any more alliteration.

to think about these questions and how they relate to your own life.

My last reason for this book is that I enjoy writing it. May you derive as much joy and inspiration from reading it as I do from writing it.

CHAPTER 2

Core Beliefs

"I am not good enough."

"I don't belong."

"I have to pretend I am different in order to get their approval."

These were my core beliefs. They formed the basis of my relationship with the world and totally dominated my life. They structured my experience and were so ingrained that I didn't see them as beliefs, but as absolute truths.

As young children, our entire survival is dependent on our parents. We must please them. We try to be who we think they want us to be. We reach erroneous conclusions about our role in the world and cling to them tenaciously.

When I was about four years old, I often played in a local playground near the apartment house where we lived. One day stands out in my memory, when an older boy said to me, "You're cross-eyed!" Hating to be seen as different, I denied it vehemently even though I was profoundly cross-eyed. It was so extreme that my right eye pointed toward my nose when my left eye looked ahead. Was this event the source of my core belief that I did not belong, or had it been formed at an earlier age? I don't know.

When I was five, this condition was partially corrected surgically, so that I was then only moderately cross-eyed. When I was a teenager, I underwent surgery again. Since then I have been only slightly cross-eyed, and most people don't notice it. Nevertheless, I still lack normal depth perception, and my compromised vision became the source of many painful episodes when I was young.

During childhood, for instance, my older brother and I were sent to a summer camp which stressed competition and athletics. Imagine trying to hit a softball without depth perception! My memories of sporting occasions were riddled with feelings of embarrassment and failure. One of my more painful memories involves how teams were chosen when playing softball. The counselors picked two team captains, who then alternately chose someone until the final person was chosen. I was usually the next-to-last chosen because a kid whose left arm was paralyzed and shrunken was usually the last. I remember one particular day when he was up to bat. He held the bat

8

with one hand and connected solidly with the ball, slamming it far over the second baseman's head. I felt devastated, my own sense of inadequacy driven home even deeper by his success.

Even though I held strongly to my core beliefs for the first 60 years of my life, there were many experiences which could have provided contrary evidence. For example, as a child I had a best friend and several other friends. Each day, three of us would walk together to and from school. After school, I would play with many kids in the immediate neighborhood. I was told I was smart. As a teenager, I was elected president of a local ham radio club. But until about ten years ago, my fundamental experience of the world was that I did not belong. I was mostly oblivious to any evidence which contradicted this internal feeling of alienation. In my mind, I was a social outcast, a stranger, and an exception. I was born in Brooklyn, N.Y., but I felt like an alien on planet Earth.

When I was eleven or twelve, my father enrolled me in acting school. He wanted to cure my stuttering and increase my self-confidence. The class met each Saturday morning in Manhattan, a few blocks from Broadway. Soon my father's plan began to work, but not in the way he intended. The training I received gave me the means to camouflage myself. From that time on, I felt that I could successfully pretend to be part of the crowd, and nobody would know that I did not belong. I learned to perform with some adroitness on the stage, both at the acting school and in the game of life. I discovered that I could bluff my way through life by pretending to be normal.

We all entertain some form of the belief that we are not good enough. Perhaps we believe we are not smart enough or attractive enough, or skilled enough. Many seekers believe they are not spiritual enough. Like most people, I had no idea that almost everybody believes some version of "I am not good enough."

During my teenage years, I became interested in girls. That was no great surprise. What was a huge surprise, a complete shock, was that girls were interested in me. I could not understand it. It made no sense at all that these girls were unable to discern that I was not a worthy match.

At the age of fifteen, I spent the summer at a camp for teenagers. In the mornings, we worked on some project, such as construction, lumbering, or gardening; afternoons were spent on cultural activities; and evenings usually involved some entertainment. The boys and girls tended to pair up. During the first week, a very pretty, outgoing girl wanted to pair up with me. But I knew with absolute certainty that she would soon dump me. Why go through that pain? I avoided her until she finally gave up and found someone more popular and outgoing.

Like most people, I had no idea that my belief of not being good enough was common. I didn't know that I could question this belief, begin to appreciate my life much more deeply, and even learn to love myself. Without awareness, I accepted the truth of my self-assessment and let it dictate most of my decisions.

Decades became structured by choices made from my sense of inferiority and alienation.

By this time, I had developed some other core beliefs, namely, "I am smarter than all of them" and "because I am smarter, cleverer, and shrewder, I will succeed."

I received a merit-based college scholarship that could be used anywhere in New York State. I was accepted by Cornell University, a prestigious Ivy-League college, which my older brother had attended. Most men at Cornell joined fraternities, and I knew that no fraternity would want me. So I chose instead to go to the University of Rochester where most men lived in dorms.

At Rochester I had friends and some happy times. During my first year there, I met my first girlfriend, Marjie. It took several years, but it eventually sunk into my consciousness that somebody I found attractive actually liked me. After Marjie, I had another girlfriend at Rochester and, little by little, I gave up my belief that I was unattractive to women. But instances of "I'm not good enough" are generally hard to drop, even in the face of countervailing evidence. I still believed myself to be an alien and outsider, but I was one who could attract some women on this hostile planet.

I did well in mathematics, decided to become an actuary, and accepted a fellowship at the University of Michigan for two-year master's program in actuarial mathematics. As part of the program, students were encouraged to take summer jobs at life insurance companies to get some experience, while the companies evaluated the students as prospective hires. In the summer after my first year at Michigan, I worked at the Mutual Benefit Life Insurance Company in Newark, New Jersey. I anticipated that the quietness of actuarial life would suit me. To my dismay, however, I discovered that working at a life insurance company involved significant social interaction: having lunch with colleagues and bosses, attending parties, perhaps even playing golf. I knew that I could not survive in such an environment, and so I abandoned my plans to become an actuary.

Instead, I decided to pursue a Ph. D. in mathematics and become a professor. One great thing about math was that it is either correct or not. It requires no smiling to convince anyone you are correct, no politics, and no social interaction. Mathematics was, in other words, a great place for me to hide. In view of my success at the acting school, I knew I could stand in front of a class and teach, and my alienation from society would not be an impediment to doing mathematical research. So I completed a Ph.D. in mathematics, writing a dissertation in the interface between actuarial science and statistics.

I knew I would eventually want to settle down and marry. I also knew that once I left Michigan and became a professor, I would have little opportunity to meet eligible women. I was shy and unlikely to have a large circle of friends in the future. I did not visit bars or join clubs, and internet dating didn't exist then. I realized I would either have to remain a bachelor or find a wife before I completed my Ph.D.

I devised a strategy to mine the rich resources—intelligent women—available to me at Michigan. Methodically, I listed my criteria for a mate. Then I contrived a plan to meet a large number of such women, to increase my odds of finding the right one. I had met a guy who was two years younger than I and who had graduated from a large Detroit high school, many of whose graduates were now undergraduates at the University of Michigan. We would go through the photos in his high school senior yearbook to identify women who met my criteria and who were on campus. I would telephone them using the line, "You don't know me, but Jeff gave me your name." I would then invite them for a coffee date, a short afternoon encounter in the Student Union, which was relatively risk-free for both parties. Initially, it was terrifyingly difficult to telephone these women. But given the alternative of a lifetime of lonely bachelorhood, I managed to discipline myself to make one coffee date a week. With practice, making the calls became easier, and my fear of rejection diminished.

My mate-finding scheme still had a fundamental problem: How could I mate with someone belonging to a culture to which I felt so alien? One evening I met a loquacious girl named Lenore and I used the opportunity to further my wife-quest by covertly asking her about her friends. Among the people she mentioned was Carol Shulman, whom she described as a friendly, warm, caring person, who was very shy and withdrawn. "Hmm," I thought, "perhaps here's someone even shyer than I." So I pumped Lenore for information about Carol to determine whether Carol met my criteria. She did, and I added Carol to my list of potential coffee dates.

Not only was Carol shy, but she was sexy, pretty, and very smart. She was also creative and fun to be with. Would we be two alien souls? Would Carol be a bridge between me and this foreign world?

It sounds odd, but it is true: I do not remember my coffee date with Carol. I also do not remember our first "real" date. Even after that date, I dated Carol occasionally while continuing my coffee dates and "real" dates with others. There was no lightning from the sky and no violins. Our love developed slowly. A year and a half later, Carol and I became a couple. Another year passed and we were engaged, and another half-year later we were married.

Now, forty-six years later, I still cannot believe how fortunate I am to have my wonderful wife by my side. I love Carol more deeply than I ever imagined I could love another person. Although she has not pursued the same path as I in the quest for happiness, she has always supported me. Marrying her was the best decision I have ever made. She is truly my life partner. I am so very grateful that an immature twenty-one-year old decided to methodically seek a mate.

My career as a mathematics professor was a success. I wrote many research papers and mentored six doctoral students. My colleagues treated me as normal, but my belief in my social inadequacy—my feeling that I did not and never would belong—

persisted. Furthermore, I was correct in anticipating that I would be evaluated professionally based on my research and teaching, not on my ability to make friends and be sociable. Parties and other social gatherings were infrequent, and there was no penalty for not attending. I was well suited to academic life.

Many departments of a university have one group of faculty at odds with another. Our department of mathematical sciences was especially fractious because it contained three separate areas: applied mathematics, computer science, and statistics, all competing for resources. While being detached from the world meant having no friends, it also meant having no enemies. So when we needed a new department head, I was the obvious candidate. At age 37, I assumed supervisory responsibility for 15 full-time faculty, 19 part-time faculty, 29 graduate teaching assistants, and three secretaries.

I was a fairly effective department head: I kept the peace among the warring factions and prevented the departure of some valuable faculty. But I was an emotional wreck. I was victim of the need for other peoples' approval. I could sometimes deny an individual faculty member's request by explaining that our resources were limited. On the other hand, if a conflict arose when the faculty was assembled together, I would have to take a position and risk the animosity of these alien creatures. I solved this problem by never scheduling a single faculty meeting.

Other problems were not solved as easily. As department head, I had to make decisions which would displease some people. For example, somebody has to teach at an inconvenient time. A fixed pool of salary raise money must be allocated among the other 14 faculty. Even worse, a young assistant professor must be denied tenure. Fortunately, I had the good sense to resign as department head after many maddening months of monumental misery.

Perhaps my sense of alienation was extreme. But many people's versions of not being good enough dominate their lives. These versions may take many different forms. But once they attach themselves to these beliefs, they blindly continue their allegiance to them. As an extreme example, consider anorexics who are wasting away while still believing "I am not thin enough." No matter how much weight they lose, they still believe they are not thin enough. Another example is seekers who believe they are not spiritual enough. No matter how "spiritual" they become, they still believe they are not spiritual enough.

My belief of not being good enough operated alongside my belief of being better than others. While these two beliefs are vastly different, they represent two sides of the same coin. The one was a compensator for the other. I dealt with the pain of being an outsider by telling myself I was better than others. But the effect of both was the same: distancing me from people and making me unhappy.

Some people feel superior by believing they have more insightful political views. For others, it is their faith that makes them "holier" and wiser than others. I felt superior believing I was more intelligent. I thought of myself as much smarter than other people, and this was a view at least partly founded on what I now find to be a humorously limited idea of what constitutes intelligence.

I recognized just two kinds of smartness when I was younger. The first kind involved being subtle, strategic, and savvy. To get me to the hospital for my first eye surgery, my parents said I was going to visit a sick cousin, even convincing me to bring my favorite toy in case she wanted to play with it. When I first discovered the truth, I felt stupid for having been duped, so much so that I resolved never to be fooled again. I decided that I needed to be shrewd, skeptical, and suspicious, never taking things at face value. I developed a sense of superiority over those who seemed naïve or gullible. My favorite childhood insult, often accompanied by a sneer, was "He's so simple that he thinks asphalt is rectum trouble."

I have since wholeheartedly forgiven my parents for this deception. I have learned about a deeper level forgiveness, which I will describe and illustrate in Chapter 6.

The only other kind of smartness I acknowledged as legitimate and worthwhile was mathematical acumen. As far as I was concerned, no other ability or skill counted. Someone who could write poetry, compose music, make philosophical distinctions, speak foreign languages, or create art was skilled, but not necessarily smart in my view. As I met others who were also gifted mathematically, I restricted my notion of "smart" even further, confining my criterion for

17

mathematical smartness to particular branches of mathematics.

As a Ph.D. student at Michigan, I did well in math classes, but I was not exceptional. I really excelled in real analysis, measure theory, and probability theory. Accordingly, I honed my version of "I'm smarter than you" into "I'm smarter than anyone in these areas of mathematics." I felt that unless others excelled similarly, they were inferior. I believed I had a special insight into these areas of mathematics.

Many years later, I met someone whose mathematical smartness, even as I had so narrowly defined it, clearly exceeded mine. This discovery was immensely liberating and comforting. It meant that I was no longer unique—no longer a freak. With this increased awareness, I allowed myself to recognize several other people whose mathematical acumen exceeded mine. No doubt, I was mathematically gifted, but I no longer considered myself mathematically extraordinary. These days I see this awakening as a necessary precursor to dropping the belief "I am better than you because I am smarter," as it made me realize how I had been unconsciously managing my world.

My beliefs in my inadequacy and superiority interacted in strange ways. For example, I did not think my doctoral dissertation was especially strong. So I employed what I thought was shrewdness and guile to make it more appealing. A mathematical expression can either be included inline with the text or displayed centered on a separate line. I chose the latter whenever possible to increase the apparent length of the 54-page dissertation. Also, even though I was solving an applied problem, I tried to impress the theoreticians on my committee by couching the dissertation in the theoretical format of theorems followed by proofs and by adding unnecessary abstraction. In retrospect, it is clear that these tactics were totally unnecessary. In fact, my research paper based on the dissertation was required reading for actuarial students for more than twenty years.

When I was in college, I categorized some people as inferior depending on the sound of their voice. I associated a Brooklyn accent with stupidity, and I felt the same about Southern accents. So when I arrived at Rochester, I worked diligently to lose all vestiges of my own Brooklyn accent. Years later, as a professor at Florida State University, I was shocked by the incongruity of hearing mathematical terms pronounced with a Southern accent. It took quite a while to become accustomed to it. Now, having lived in Texas for over thirty years, I no longer associate speech patterns with intelligence. *Y'all un'stan'?*

I felt superior to those who did not appreciate puns and other clever word-plays. I also felt superior to people who are superstitious or believe in items for which I think there is no objective evidence, such as astrology, fundamentalist religion, and homeopathy. I also believed that people in America who are shrewd and bright should be at least moderately wealthy, so I felt superior to poor people, judging them as stupid. Having discovered how to become wealthy as an entrepreneur, I felt smugly superior to my colleagues who were living solely off their salaries as professors.

I have described childhood events which may have caused some of my beliefs. Were they really the cause? Perhaps my beliefs were inculcated earlier and I can recall only those incidents which reinforced them. What is the significance of the fact that I remember some events and not others? To what extent did my older brother teach me the beliefs in my inadequacy? I do not know the answers to those questions, and I do not need to know. I have not found it useful to identify the source of my beliefs.

Thoughts of the "I'm not good enough" variety are totally dysfunctional. Believing them made me unhappy. Worse, they caused me to lie, deceive, and pretend, fearing that others might discover my inferiority and reject me as I rejected myself. I then added to my feelings of unworthiness by feeling guilty for my lying, deception, and pretense. Without the opposing beliefs of "I'm better than you," I could have spiraled downward into a virtual self-created hell on earth. These opposing beliefs were my lifelines out of hell, providing me some momentary relief from my misery. But both kinds made it hard to respect, love, and accept myself.

Many people live their entire lives believing versions of the thoughts "I'm not good enough" and "I'm better than you." I have deep compassion for these people because I know how much they suffer. I suffered too. Most of them know no alternative. They have not yet taken the first step out of hell, which is to know that they are in hell—a self-created hell.

We do not perceive events directly. Instead, we view life through the filters of our beliefs, and we frequently misinterpret events. We notice and remember those events which reinforce our beliefs and often ignore those which contradict them. Many of our beliefs about ourselves, which we learned as very young children, are false.

It has me taken time and perseverance to learn not to believe thoughts of the form "I'm not good enough" and "I'm better than you." I will describe my efforts in detail later in this book. Believing versions of "I'm not good enough" makes us unhappy and diminishes our self-love. Believing versions of "I'm better than you" gives us momentary pleasure, but ultimately makes us unhappy by separating ourselves from others and denying them love and acceptance. I still have thoughts of "I'm not good enough" and "I'm better than you," but I have learned to doubt them. I question them as they arise. As I slowly free myself from these thoughts, my happiness increases. I love myself more, I love others more, and I enjoy life more.

We can also lessen the hold of the beliefs in our inferiority and superiority by reminding ourselves that abilities or disabilities do not determine self-worth. My being smarter than you in no way implies that I am better than you, just as your being stronger than me, or able to speak Lithuanian, or being capable of producing gourmet meals does not make you better than me. People are different. We can celebrate and enjoy these differences.

We all form beliefs in early childhood about who we are. Although these beliefs can be based on scanty evidence, they are strong enough to determine the course of our lives. We practice and practice until we master the art of being who we think we are. For many decades, I was an expert at being a competent, strong, independent, intelligent, outsider—a misfit intent on proving that I would succeed. I was convinced that I needed to pretend in order to gain acceptance and approval.

I still see myself as different from other people: I am reserved, shy, and introverted; I don't have many friends; I am intellectual and analytical; I don't enjoy sports or TV.

But I am totally content with who I am. I no longer believe that I am a misfit.

My daily experience is of being at home in the world and at peace. I am certainly more skilled at certain things and less at others. For example, I am proficient at playing the piano and doing mathematics, but not at writing poetry or engaging in small talk. My self-worth no longer depends on what skills or abilities I have.

I love and accept myself exactly as I am.

Recently, I was staying at a guesthouse for a few days while attending a meeting. One evening, a party was scheduled. I still don't like parties, especially with people I don't know well, but I decided to go. Small groups of people stood around talking, and a few were watching TV. I was standing alone at the snack table when I suddenly realized that I was not the same person as a few years ago. Although I am still shy and withdrawn, I was calm, comfortable, and content. Standing alone not talking to anybody was perfectly okay. In the past I would have feared what others thought about my being alone. I would have left or forced myself to join some group. Now, I could choose to join a group in conversation, I could stand by myself snacking, or I could return to my room and read a book.

I am free.

CHAPTER 3

Getting What We Want

Make a list of things you have created & made you happy.

On Sunday, September 13, 1972, at 5:16 A.M., I sat anxiously waiting at the Tallahassee Memorial Hospital maternity ward. My wife and I had planned to have only two children and she had just been brought to the delivery room to give birth to our second child. Back then, husbands were not allowed in the delivery room. I didn't know the sex of our baby because sonograms were not yet available. I loved and cherished my four-year-old daughter, but I really wanted my last child to be a boy. If I had a son, I "knew" that my life's dream would be fulfilled and that I would be happy the rest of my life. So imagine my elation when I was told at 5:22 A.M. that my wife had just delivered a healthy baby boy! I was ecstatic. Only with difficulty could I suppress tears of joy. (Men weren't supposed to cry.) For a few weeks, I was euphoric. But then, my happiness level reverted to what it had been before the birth of my son.

Given that I now had everything I had ever wanted, I had expected to continue feeling joyous. The fact was, I didn't. And that was not because I am different from most other people. It was because of a tremendously important truth: getting what we want will not make us lastingly happy. Having more money will not make us happy. Receiving admiration and adulation will not make us happy. Being loved and respected will not make us happy. Finding that perfect relationship will not make us happy. Ridding ourselves of the relationship we have found will not make us happy. GETTING EVERYTHING WE WANT WILL NOT MAKE US HAPPY.

How would my life have been different had I read a book thirty years ago emphasizing that getting what we want will not make us happy? You might be surprised to learn that I know the answer to that question. I know it because I did read such a book, *Handbook to Higher Consciousness* (Keyes, 1975). That book planted a seed in my mind, but I needed to accumulate sufficient examples in my life before that seed sprouted. My goal in this chapter is to plant that seed in your mind and water that seed with examples from my own life, hoping you will fertilize it with examples from yours.

Your reaction to the idea that getting what you want is not the key to happiness may vary widely depending on your experience and your belief system. Some people may find this statement obvious, hardly worth spending a chapter on. Others may know on some level that it is true, although they continue to pursue happiness through getting what they want. (I was in this category for several decades.) Still others may feel incredulous, and find this statement impossible to accept because it conflicts so strongly with what they have been taught and always believed. That is not surprising. There are many good reasons why it can be hard to accept the idea that getting what you want does not make you happy.

The book I read about happiness did not have an immediate effect on me because its message was at odds with much of the rest of what I thought I knew. Like all of us, I was inundated with the notion that improving my circumstances would make me happy. Our entire culture is oriented toward that idea: get an education, find a good job, get married, have children. Advertisements imply that their product or service will make us happy. We are constantly bombarded by such messages from our parents, teachers, and friends. If a lie is repeated often enough people will believe it, and this lie is being drilled into our minds incessantly. Given the pervasiveness of the lie that changing our circumstances will make us happy, it is very difficult to realize the truth.

Little children live in the moment. They do not exhibit any desire to plan for the future or to be productive citizens. That desire has to be instilled into them, and instilled it is. We are told that without it, children will never succeed. Their parents try to motivate them by promising future happiness. Without this promise, parents fear their children will not aspire to goals and ambitions, will not get an education, and will not be creative or productive. Without this incentive, they fear for their children: some fear their kids will just smoke pot and collect welfare; others fear that the kids will never leave home and make it on their own. However these fears become configured, they are unfounded, and they perpetuate the belief that getting something we want that we do not have right now will make us happy. This false belief is as a carrot forever dangling in front of us. By saying this, I am not implying that our parents are to blame. They learned these fears from their parents and teachers, who in turn learned them from earlier generations. My point here is that this future-oriented idea of how to be happy pervades our culture and deprives us of the chance to find true happiness.

Like many untruths, the idea that changing circumstances can make us happy also contains a small element of truth. Every time I got what I wanted, I did experience at least some short-term pleasure. I was euphoric when my son was born, elated when I was promoted from assistant professor to associate professor, and thrilled when promoted to full professor. But after the short-term pleasure wore off, I was no happier as a full professor than I had been as an assistant professor. Are college presidents generally happier than the people who clean their offices at night? I suspect not.

The rush that we feel when we get what we want is addictive. Each time we succeed, we experience an ephemeral, fleeting emotional high, similar to a drug addict's high from each hit or snort. So, like a drug addict, we fervently seek the next emotional high. With drugs, the addiction has an enormous cost. Although our addiction to seeking happiness by satisfying our desires is not as debilitating as a drug addiction, it also extracts costs.

One cost of this addiction is our inability to enjoy the present moment. With our attention riveted on the next goal we think will make us happy, we rob ourselves of the pleasure of celebrating, loving, and enjoying the current moment. Yet, now is all there is. Anytime we entertain the thought, "I will be happy when...," we are missing the opportunity to savor the beauty of life right now.

This addiction entails another cost. Failing to achieve the happiness we expect, we may feel discouraged and hopeless, resigning ourselves to a joyless life. Even worse, we often blame ourselves for this failure and feel dejected and powerless.

Let's try a brief exercise. First, imagine that I am placing my mouth close to your left ear, as if to whisper something important to you. Take a moment and picture it. Pause for a moment. Now, when you are ready, imagine that, instead of whispering, I shout as loudly as I can, "Getting what you want will not make you happy!" Imagine that this message reverberates throughout your skull, so that you never forget it.

Those whose thinking is punctilious, pedantic, and precise might object that if what we want is to be happy, then getting what we want will, of course, make us happy. I will concede the point because changing the way we think, modifying how we look at the world, and adopting an attitude of gratitude can indeed make us happy. So my statement needs to be modified by specifying that getting what we want in the sense of changing the external circumstances in our life will not make us happy.

We can certainly become happier or at least less unhappy by improving certain external circumstances. Yet these changes cannot lead to lasting happiness, contentment, satisfaction, and peace of mind. For example, people engaged in meaningful work are probably happier than those who are not. People who have a loving circle of family or friends tend to be happier than those who do not. The same is true for people having the opportunity to express their creativity. But I know from my own personal experience that having all these things did not make me truly happy.

Wouldn't we be happier if we had more money, perhaps additional funds to spend on vacations or objects that might bring us pleasure? Surprisingly, the answer is no. Most studies show that increased income does not result in increased happiness after basic needs are provided for. I found this result surprising, since I had spent much of my life trying to become wealthier. If increased wealth caused increased happiness, then people who won the lottery would certainly be happier. But many well-designed studies have consistently shown exactly the opposite. Shortly after winning, lottery winners were euphoric, but after a period of time, these people were no happier than before.

Being skeptical of psychological research and having training in statistics, I searched the literature carefully to evaluate the primary sources. I verified that the result was well-established by research dating back to 1978. For example, Brickman, Coates, and Janoff-Bulman (1978) state: "Study 1 compared a sample of 22 major lottery winners with 22 controls.... Lottery winners were not happier than controls and took significantly less pleasure from a series of mundane events. Study 2, using 86 Ss who lived close to past lottery winners, indicated that these effects were not due to preexisting differences between people who buy or do not buy lottery tickets...." A fairly recent article (Lutter, 2007) summarized the situation as follows: "Winning the lottery has no significant positive or negative effect on happiness....Winners are not happier or unhappier than before or than non-winners. After a period of peak experience, winners return back to their prior level of happiness."

If more money won't make us happier, what about prestige, fame, and approval? In my experience, these do not increase happiness either. There are two problems with seeking prestige, fame, and approval as a path to increased happiness. The first is that no matter how much we get, it is never enough. Fortunately, I was not as attracted to these attributes as I was to money, but I can share some experiences and observations. Shortly after getting a Ph.D., I enjoyed the prestige, but that pleasure dissipated fairly quickly, for I now sought approval and prestige from my colleagues, all of whom had Ph.D.'s. Also, I resented the fact that M.D.'s had more prestige than Ph.D.'s. I also noticed many of my colleagues were constantly driven to publish more and more in pursuit of increased prestige. Instead of resting on their laurels, they felt pressured to keep going but appeared no happier for doing so.

A second problem is that seeking prestige, fame, and approval as a path to happiness attempts to cure the problem without addressing its cause. People who love and accept themselves exactly as they are do not need the approval of others. Their self-love and self-approval are more than sufficient. Consider the most successful actors and athletes: people who have achieved outstanding success in their fields. Now that they have acquired prestige, fame, and approval, are they happier? If we can believe the popular press, it does not appear so. In fact, a study in the 1990's (Fowles, 1992, pp. ix and 238) found a much higher suicide rate among 100 "people who have achieved great fame in the United States as performers" than in the general population.

Some people seek power as a means toward happiness. Yet, no matter how much power they acquire, they always crave more. A regional manager of a company may think she will be happier as vice president; a vice-president may need to be president and chairman of the board. Instead of stopping there, many individuals in that position then go on to acquire other companies in order to be more powerful. Many politicians continually seek higher office. It seems that these people are addicted to power. Our commerce and political systems would be transformed if people realized that happiness cannot be found through acquiring power.

The birth of my son was but one of numerous instances throughout my life when I "knew" that I would be truly happy if I got what I wanted. I then got what I wanted, but, after the initial pleasure wore off, was not much happier. Other instances were getting my amateur radio license at age 13, acquiring my first car, and passing the preliminary exams for the Ph.D.

I always wanted to own my own home. In 1970, Carol and I bought a house in Tallahassee, Florida on one-half acre of land. For the first few weeks, I would strut around the perimeter of the yard, thinking "This is mine. It is really mine." But after a short while, I was no happier.

At one point, Carol and I had marital problems. I "knew" I would be happy once they were resolved. After they were resolved, I was only slightly happier.

Beginning in 1996, I was afflicted with spinal stenosis, where a narrowing of my lumbar spine put pressure on the nerves serving my legs, causing numbness whenever I stood up straight. I could not stand or walk erect for more than a few minutes, but I could walk leaning forward and supported by a shopping cart or even a foreshortened cane. When I needed to walk, I used a walker, modified by adding two more wheels. Several spine surgeons indicated that they could repair the problem, but the surgery required removing bone from my hip and using it to fuse one joint in my spine, putting more stress on the other joints. Some of the surgeons recommended that the fusion be reinforced by rods and screws. I decided to wait until a more promising solution arose, and continued in the meantime with my slightly disabled lifestyle.

After five years, I found a surgeon in another city who had developed a microsurgical procedure to correct the problem without removing bone from my hip and without fusion. A few hours after recovering from the anesthesia, I was encouraged to walk. And walk, I did. I walked from my hospital room to the end of the hall, and back to my room, and back to the end of the hall, and back to my room, repeating this circuit many times. Although I experienced some pain from the surgery, I was amazed that I could walk again like a normal human being. When I arrived home two days later, I went to a local supermarket and walked up and down every aisle. I was grateful that I could walk normally again and I was thankful that I had not taken the advice of the earlier surgeons. I enjoyed several amazingly glorious weeks of being able to walk normally. But, in retrospect, I was no happier in the years immediately following the surgery than during the five years with spinal stenosis.

Another example was my early retirement from the University. I had tested retirement by taking a year's leave of absence during which I discovered that I could earn more money and have more fun by managing my part-time business. So I decided to make the next year at the University my last. Universities generally welcome the retirement of a tenured full professor so they can hire new faculty at less cost. Knowing this, I was able to negotiate a favorable deal in return for my voluntary retirement at age 55. Some professors retire gradually, but I quit cold-turkey. I gave away all my books, discarded all correspondence, and only retained a copy of each paper I wrote and each dissertation I directed. No more driving to and from work, searching for a parking space, grading exams, or useless faculty meetings. I was now free. I could expand my business, retain it at its current level, or end it. I was free to enjoy the fruit of my many years of hard work, astute financial planning and thrifty nest egg building. Although I was happier than before, I still did not experience the lasting joy, satisfaction, and peace of mind that I suspected was possible.

The story was the same when, three years ago, I developed sciatica, a painful condition which was relieved only when I sat or lay down in a fetal position. I remember predicting that once my sciatica disappeared, I would be truly happy, joyful, and serene. Sciatica tends to resolve over time, and it slowly improved. I was much happier without pain, but its disappearance did not result in the serenity and joy that I had expected.

Some people may be so focused on immediate pleasure that they do not adequately plan for the future, but I have not met anybody like this. The people I know, including myself, tend to make the opposite error of preparing for the future at the expense of enjoying the present. A mother might say to her six-year-old son: "You need to study hard in school in order to get into a top high school. Getting into a good high school will help you gain admission to a top university. Attendance at a top university is important to get a good job. You need a good job to earn lots of money. Lots of money will allow you to accumulate a sufficient sum at retirement to get into a good nursing home. Then you can be happy for the last five years of your life." Although this monologue is fictitious, farcical, and facetious, this lesson was taught to me as a child. My parents never spoke those words, but they communicated this lesson implicitly. They demonstrated it themselves by continually preparing for the future and never enjoying the present. Until I gained sufficient awareness, I spent the first 65 years of my life on this treadmill, looking forward to my future happiness with the thought, "I will be happy in the future when…."

I am continually grateful for a loving wife, two wonderful children, financial independence, good health, three beautiful grandchildren, and a safe and secure environment. But I now know that they are not the source of my happiness. You might be tempted to conclude that anyone favored with these circumstances would be happy, but you would be mistaken. For many years, I had all of these things (except for the grandchildren), but I was not especially happy. And I know many others, similarly fortunate, who are not especially happy.

This chapter explained why seeking to satisfy our desires is not an effective prescription for happiness. In the next chapter, I will explain why the most effective path to true happiness, joy, satisfaction, and peace of mind is to change our thoughts, beliefs, and points of view, rather than our external circumstances. Should you decide to pursue this path, don't expect your life to change suddenly. Habitual thought patterns are like a massive ocean liner steaming steadily straight ahead, while this chapter is only a slight force acting on the ship's bow, turning the ship imperceptibly. The momentum of the ship will continue to propel it in almost the same direction. But the force of this chapter may grow, continually turning the ship more and more as time passes.

Knowledge is not sufficient to effect transformation. Have you ever done something which you knew was not in your best interests? In order to break his habit, a drug addict first needs to acknowledge that he has an addiction. But that understanding is not sufficient for him to overcome his addiction. Similarly, my initial recognition that changed circumstances do not lead to happiness was not sufficient to cure my addiction to seeking happiness where it cannot be found. It took me over five years of diligent study and practice to change my habitual way of thinking, and this process is still ongoing. I'll tell you later how I did it.

Despite having stopped sprinting after the carrot of future happiness, I am as motivated as ever, and much more fulfilled. For instance, it feels wonderful to write this book, even though finding the right words and organizing my thoughts are sometimes challenging. I want people to read it and derive value from it in the future, and I am motivated by that desire, but my enjoyment is now.

CHAPTER 4

Wake-up Calls:
Becoming a Seeker

Suppose your boss never appreciates anything you do. Your accomplishments are never enough. Rather than acknowledge you for doing a good job, she always claims that you should have done better. She is never satisfied. You feel bitter, indignant, and resentful. But sometimes you think perhaps she's right and you feel discouraged, frustrated, and dejected—a very unhappy situation. Is it correct to say that your unappreciative boss (the external event) is causing your unhappiness (the emotional response)? Notice that there are other elements here: your interpretation of the event, your point of view, and the story you tell yourself about the event. The causal chain actually looks as follows:

[External event]
⬇
[Interpretation, story, point of view]
⬇
[Emotional response]

Someone else in the same situation, but with a different set of concerns based on a different history, might perceive things quite differently. He might be confident that he is doing an excellent job and simply ignore her criticism. If the boss is equally demanding of herself, he could have compassion for the suffering and stress she causes to herself. Alternatively, he could be thankful for having a job he enjoys doing with friendly coworkers and good pay, while viewing the boss as only a minor irritant. The interpretations we bring to the events in our lives play a crucial part in how we experience the world.

Intellectually, I understood this point decades ago, but only recently have I come to recognize its practical import. Because interpretation does, indeed, play such a pivotal role in determining our happiness, being able to change our interpretation of an event allows us to change our world.

When I was a young man, my wife and I would sometimes visit my parents for dinner, after which the four of us would play bridge. After a while, my father would say "George is getting tired. Let's quit soon." I resented that he thought so little of me that he used me as an excuse, rather than admitting that he was tired and wanted to quit soon. If I denied being tired, he would reply, "Yes, you are. I can see it in your eyes." Then I felt demeaned and insulted, because I felt treated like a child.

It was obvious to my wife, though not to me, that my upsets were caused not by my father's actions, but by my interpretations, which were perhaps influenced by memories of past childhood incidents. I was invested emotionally in my father's treating me in a way that I deemed respectful, and then got upset when he did not match my expectations. I can see this now because, over time, I stopped believing in these stories I was telling myself. My father continued to declare that I was fading at the end of an evening, but I stopped taking his remarks personally, and just saw them as his unskilled way of saying that he was tired. Eventually, I even came to see humor in the situation.

We will always experience adverse events over which we have little control, ranging from rude drivers to corrupt politicians to war mongers. Although unable to change these events, we have a choice of how we interpret them and whether we take them personally. We can accept the reality that some drivers are rude and some are polite. Some politicians are corrupt, while others are honest and hardworking. Some people promote violence and warfare, while many others are committed to the goal of world peace. We can rave, rant, and rebel over injustice and be miserable, or we can tell a different story.

Here is another example showing that my stories, not the external events, cause my emotional response.

A few nights ago, my wife served a delicious homemade espresso pound cake with cranberries and hazelnuts. Before going to sleep, I ate a piece of the leftover cake, after which I took another. After promising myself not to eat any more, I ate the last piece. I then felt guilt and remorse. What was the cause of my emotional response? Surely, it was not the fact that I ate the cake after promising myself that I wouldn't. That external circumstance no longer existed. All that existed at that time to cause my emotional response were my recollection of the event and the story I told about it—the thoughts that I should not have eaten so much cake, that I should keep promises to myself, and that I need to learn more self-control.

Frequently, rather than enjoying the present moment, the mind is concerned with some past event, and these thoughts fill us with fear, guilt, or even self-loathing. We mull over what could have happened or what we think should have happened. We make ourselves miserable by reliving events that occurred in the distant past, perhaps even in childhood. We might recall times when we were happy and regret that the present does not measure up. These are examples of how unhappiness is caused by our belief system—the totality of our thoughts, beliefs, interpretations, and points of view. Because our perception of the world is filtered through our belief system, we experience a distorted view of the world—a self-created virtual reality. We have been taught from early childhood to judge ourselves harshly when we err. This critical voice of self-judgment—our inner critic—is our constant companion. Rather than enjoying the present, we listen to this voice fretting about the past—placing our attention on events having no current reality.

The mind also expends considerable energy worrying about the future. Worry is never about the present; it is always future-oriented. Worry is a counter-productive, dysfunctional way of thinking that we learned in childhood and is continually reinforced by our culture. For example, an email I received from the brokerage firm Merrill Lynch touted an article entitled "Want to Stop Worrying about Retirement?" The article begins, "Financial worries getting the best of you? By following these four steps, you can chart a steady course that may put the worst of your retirement fears to rest."

We don't perceive current reality. Instead, our experience is dominated by habitual ways of thinking determined by past judgments and imagined futures, out of which we create our virtual reality. Therefore, the most efficient path to happiness is to modify the belief system that causes our unpleasant emotions. Then our natural love, joy, and peace of mind can shine through. The question is: how can we generate this kind of transformation?

I have experimented with many techniques to disentangle myself from my inner critical voice of self-judgment, to change my belief system, and to modify my story from one of criticism and judgment to one of love for myself and others. In order to progress from where we see ourselves to be (Point A) to where we want to be (Point B), we have been taught to reject Point A and crave Point B. But that strategy is ineffective. I have discovered that what works is to love and accept myself exactly as I am while preferring Point B to Point A.

Last night, for example, I tried playing the lovely second movement of Beethoven's Piano Sonata #8 (Pathétique, Op. 13). Not having played this piece in over a year, I played it haltingly and unevenly, with many mistakes (Point A). I was pleasantly surprised that my body could still unconsciously translate the black dots on paper into finger movements on the piano. I realized that I really enjoyed playing this piece and would enjoy it even more if I could play it smoothly with few mistakes (Point B). I accepted that I could play the piece only as well as I played it, and didn't need to berate myself as motivation to learn to play it better. I decided to spend some time over the next few weeks practicing this piece until I could play it reasonably well.

Rejecting any part of yourself masks the truth that you are perfect the way you are and alienates you from the reality of the present moment. The statement, "you are perfect the way you are" may seem absurd. When I first encountered this idea, I used to get upset because I could list numerous aspects of myself that I didn't like. If this statement were true, there seemed to be no reason to change. It took me many, many years to realize it was true. Even now, there are times when my mind resists this truth. If you reject this statement, that is fine. You really are perfect the way you are, even when you deny it.

Have I now told you the secret to happiness? Is this book the ultimate self-help book that will finally make you happy? Of course not, because telling you this is insufficient. There is no manual that can teach you how to drive a car. Similarly, no amount of knowledge or insight will enable you to love yourself exactly as you are right now. I love the aphorism of Werner Erhard, the founder of *est*, who said, "In life, understanding is the booby prize." Like learning to drive a car or play a violin, learning to be happy takes time and practice.

Even though I cannot learn to drive a car from a book, a book might be useful. For example, it can advise me to steer in the direction of a skid and also offer me other tips and techniques, as well as explain the rules. Books promoting transformation can be useful reminders in a world where communication is dominated by radio, television, newspapers, and the Internet. They can point us in the right direction, but no amount of knowledge or understanding can do it for us. For most people, happiness is a learned skill requiring extensive practice. It is experiential—not based on knowledge.

Unlike learning to drive a car, learning to be happy requires much unlearning. I have had to unlearn many of the beliefs, ways of thinking, and points of view taught to me in childhood. For most of us, that unlearning takes time, practice, and more practice. I say "most of us" because there are exceptions. I know of at least three living people[4] who are said to have spontaneously become happy in an instantaneous transformational experience. In each case, these people were reputed to have hit bottom emotionally, being depressed, miserable, or even suicidal before their sudden transformation. There may be other exceptions, but, for almost everyone else, practice is the key.

In 1977 and 1980, I experienced two events, each of which had a profound effect on my experience of life. They served as wake-up calls, revealing the possibility of an aware, alert, attentive aliveness.

The first event was the *est* training, a widely popular, controversial seminar which was offered in the 1970's and early 1980's. The training took place on two consecutive weekends in a hotel ballroom with 100 to 300 participants. Each session began at 8:30 in the morning and lasted until well past midnight, with only a limited number of meal breaks and bathroom breaks. Authoritarian, dynamic instructors led the sessions and enforced a strict set of rules. The stated purpose of the *est* training was "to transform your ability to experience living so that the situations you have been putting up with or trying to change clear up just in the process of life itself."

Before doing the *est* training, I was numb to life, but didn't know it. Afterwards, I was numb, but knew it. In the Introduction to this book, I asked, "What happened to our spark, spirit, and spunk? Can this joy

---

[4] Byron Katie, Howard Raphael Cushnir, and Eckhart Tolle.

of life be revived? Why do so many of us instead experience cynicism, resignation, and discontent?" After the *est* training, I knew the answer. Paradoxically, I learned clearly in the *est* training that just knowing the answer was useless. The value of the *est* training was the short-lived experience of joy, aliveness, and bliss that followed. Even though that experience was temporary, knowing that it was possible inspired me and drove my ensuing twenty-five year quest for happiness. I was driven by the desire to experience happiness and peace as an ongoing way of being, not as an occasional peak experience.

The *est* training has often been described as an emotional roller-coaster because the participants experience and express a wide range of emotions, including rage, confusion, boredom, fear, humiliation, sorrow, hopelessness, optimism, calm, exhilaration, and liberation. My own emotional response was limited. I discovered in the *est* training the extent to which I suppressed emotions. I was brought up to believe that the mind and rationality were good, but that emotions were bad. I remember my father often getting angry and then working very hard to control his anger. As a child I consciously decided to be rational rather than emotional. By making decisions rationally, I thought I would have a great advantage over others who made decisions emotionally. After doing the *est* training, I recommended it enthusiastically to my brother. He had never seen me enthusiastic about anything, and he enrolled just because of my enthusiasm.

In the *est* training I discovered the distinction between experiencing life directly and living it conceptually. I became aware of the inner voice—the incessant, involuntary, repetitive monologue that constantly evaluates and judges ourselves and others. We often label that voice "thinking," but thinking is voluntary, while this voice is involuntary. Not only do we hear the voice, but we also identify with it; we think it is us. We rarely consider the possibility that the voice is erroneous, that its pronouncements are just reflections of beliefs taught to us as children. This was a monumental discovery for me. I was also amazed to discover the amount of time I spent listening to that voice rather than experiencing life directly.

For a few weeks after the *est* training, life was brighter. I noticed things that I hadn't noticed before: trees, grass, birds. It seemed that I perceived the world directly, without judging or evaluating what I was seeing. The experience gradually faded, but the memory of it gave me the hope that true happiness was possible. For the first time, I began to conceive of the possibility of really joining the human race rather than continuing with my pretense. My desire to stop being an alien misfit grew. I didn't know whether I was condemned to my hellish existence for the rest of my days, or if there were an escape. But I decided, with *est*'s help, to find out.

Graduates of *est* were encouraged to take advanced seminars. These graduate seminars were led by well-trained volunteers—men and women who were expressive, outgoing, and self-confident. Each candidate had to undergo extensive training before being certified to lead graduate seminars. So here was my plan: I would train to become a graduate seminar leader. I expected one of two outcomes. First, I might fail and discover that I was truly a misfit with no hope of joining the human race. But at least, I would have the satisfaction of knowing the truth. Second, I might succeed at becoming a seminar leader, find my salvation, escape from hell, and reclaim my human birthright.

My plan failed: Neither of these outcomes occurred. After extensive training, I was certified to lead graduate seminars. But I still felt like a misfit, even after leading successful seminars for several months. My wife, having attended one of my seminars, commented afterwards, "That's not the George I know." She knew the shy, mathematics professor who saw himself as a social misfit, not the expressive, friendly, intuitive, outgoing, self-confident, empathic seminar leader others saw.

Three years after the *est* training, a second event had a profound effect on my experience of life. In 1980, I did an exercise as part of a seven-day program led by Ken Keyes, Jr., author of *Handbook to Higher Consciousness* (Keyes 1975). We were divided into groups of about twenty-five people, each group sent to a separate room. Our group formed a large circle, facing into the center. The exercise was led by two facilitators, one male and one female, standing in the center with a microphone. After some introductory remarks about the body, we were suddenly directed to remove all our clothes! I could not believe they were serious until the facilitators, who I then noticed had been wearing robes, removed their robes and were naked. Seeing the other participants begin to strip, I felt I had no choice but to do the same. I had no trouble removing my socks, shirt, undershirt, and even my pants, but I felt very nervous, fearful, and anxious when I finally removed my underpants, throwing them on the pile with the rest of my clothes. Fearing that all eyes were on me, I slowly looked up, and was relieved to find that I was not the last to undress, nor was anybody watching me.

My fear intensified as each of us had to come to the center of the circle, take the microphone from the floor, and speak into it, telling which of our body parts we most and least admired. I dreaded being seen bending over to retrieve the microphone and again to replace it on the floor. Speaking into the microphone, I felt the intense discomfort of knowing that now all eyes were indeed gazing at my naked body, viewing me from every angle. But after returning to my place in the circle, I began to relax a bit. Looking around the circle, I guiltily perused the nude female bodies, noticing how they were all the same, yet all different. Despite my guilt, I realized that I enjoyed looking at them. I then viewed the male bodies. Because I was not muscular, I had not considered my body especially attractive to women. I was surprised to notice that I ranked my body among the top 25% of the male bodies in the circle.

That exercise shook me initially, but was also of great benefit. Although I was nervous, fearful, and anxious, there was no threat to me during the exercise; I was perfectly safe. Why then was I so afraid? My strong emotional reaction arose solely from my beliefs. Ever since childhood, I had believed that I shouldn't expose my body to members of the opposite sex. At that moment, I was aware of my emotions, but not the underlying belief. Now I know that my beliefs and interpretations, not what is actually happening, cause almost all of my stressful emotions. In fact, whenever I experience an unpleasant emotion, I can stop to explore the underlying beliefs and then question their validity.

That experience, besides providing a great lesson in the causes of unhappy emotions, also led to my becoming less self-conscious about my body. That exercise was the first step of my realization that bodies can be celebrated and enjoyed, not hidden, denied, or feared. If I were to do that exercise now, my experience would be entirely different. It would be fun; I would have no fear whatsoever. A body is just a body; photons reflecting off my body into someone's retina do not mean anything. I would not dread bending over to get the mic. Although it is an unattractive position and they might not like the view, it is not my problem. Also, I could enjoy viewing female bodies without guilt or shame, and would see no need to compare my body with others. As my love for my own body and my appreciation of the bodies of others has grown, so

51

has my love for my wife and our ability to be close and loving with each other.

Our culture sanctions deriving pleasure from the mind, but less so from the body, although it is less restrictive regarding bodily pleasures than when I was young. It was life-changing to realize how negative beliefs about my body prevented me from fully enjoying life. I have discovered new ways to get pleasure from my body. For example, I find it pleasurable to stroke my forearm gently from the elbow to the wrist. Interestingly, stroking in the other direction does not feel as pleasant. Another area where I have discovered sensitivity is my upper chest.

You might want to explore your body to find areas, other than the usual erogenous zones, where your body is sensitive. Be creative and have fun with your body. Find what you enjoy. Perhaps exchange massages or foot rubs with someone, because loving yourself includes loving your body. Make your body the love of your life. One way to start loving your body is to express sincere gratitude for your body. Thank specific parts of your body for functioning well physiologically, for allowing you freedom to enjoy the world, or for giving you pleasure. Also, try viewing your body unclothed in a mirror and enjoying what you see. Don't be discouraged if, at first, you find parts of your body you don't like; in the beginning, almost everybody does. I could compare my 70-year-old body to my younger body or to some body I see in an advertisement, but I don't make those comparisons. This is the only body I have. It is perfect. I love it.

mom corr

Early in my path to happiness, I kept trying to become how I thought I should be. I considered myself a cerebral, intellectual person who lacked social and physical skills. I felt that I needed to prove to myself that I could master a complex physical task requiring bodily coordination. So, in October, 1992, at age 52, I decided to learn to fly an airplane.

Three months later, having spent 54 hours flying and performing 153 takeoffs and landings in a small dual-control airplane with an instructor, it was time for my first unsupervised solo flight. I was to fly to a nearby unattended airport, land there, and then return home. That first day I flew alone was ideal for flying. The skies were clear with good visibility; winds were light and parallel to the runways. I was flying a plane I had flown many times to an airport I had frequently visited. The only difference was the absence of my instructor.

Shortly after take-off, I became extremely nervous and began shaking uncontrollably. My arms were shaking, my legs were jumpy, and I began to sweat. In order to calm myself, I checked the flight instruments to determine that everything was okay—right airspeed, right altitude, engine doing fine. I looked to the ground and saw the familiar freeway to my right, just where it ought to be. I realized that the plane was performing well, the weather was ideal, and the only problem was me, the pilot. My mind raced in an effort both to calm myself and to determine a course of action. Returning to the home airport would require communicating with Air Traffic Control, and I wasn't sure that I could talk coherently. Also, I would either have to wait in a pattern for clearance to land or to declare an emergency. (What was the emergency? A partially panicked pilot?) I saw no choice but to continue the ten minutes to my destination and do my best to land the airplane. I would end up on the ground one way or another. My plan was to land at my destination and telephone the flying school to send an instructor to fly me and their airplane home. This would be my last flight.

Even in my state of near panic, I landed the airplane safely. In retrospect, having completed 153 landings, it was unlikely that I would fail on the 154th, even with all my nervousness. After landing at my destination, I parked the airplane, waited a long while to calm down, and considered my situation. I was too embarrassed to call for help, and now that I was calm, I thought that I could safely fly back home, but this would be my last flight. I wouldn't have to explain anything. I would just not schedule another lesson. Clearly, flying was not for me.

It wasn't my last flight. Although the FAA requires a minimum of 40 hours before taking a flight test with an FAA examiner, most students require from 50 to 70 hours before they are ready. Because of my difficulty in learning to land properly, perhaps due to my lack of normal stereoscopic depth perception, it took me 100 hours before I was finally licensed as a pilot in June of 1993.

But getting my pilot's license was not good enough. I discovered that trying to appease my inner critical voice is futile because it will simply raise the bar. To prove that I was competent in tasks involving coordination and physical accomplishment, my new challenge became obtaining an instrument rating, allowing me to fly through clouds and in conditions of limited visibility. Although I got my instrument rating, I never used it. After two more short flights, I have never piloted an airplane again. I am grateful that I learned to fly. It was exhilarating to do something I never dreamed I could do, but I now recognize that attempting to appease my inner critic will not lead to happiness.

Instead of trying to change myself, I am learning not to believe the stories I tell. Denying what I really believed and trying to convince myself to believe something different have never worked for me. Rather than trying to change me or my thoughts, what has worked for me is to accept reality as it is, a much more effective and loving technique. I notice my thoughts without trying to change them. For example, after eating the cake, I had the thought, "I need more self-control." I can hear it, acknowledge it as a thought, and then begin to doubt it by asking myself whether it is true. I don't view it as a bad thought or a negative thought; it's just a thought. Recognizing that the thought is not true, I don't feel guilty about having eaten the cake. It took me time to learn to be aware of my thoughts, and to realize that I am not my thoughts. With practice, I am learning more and more not to believe them.

Many people use meditation, either guided or unguided, as a tool on their pathway to happiness. Like other tools, it can be used or misused. Meditation has been useful to me in breaking the identification I have had with my thoughts. Over the years, I have used various types of meditation. My current technique, which may change next week or next month, is to sit quietly, breathe slowly and deeply, and then just listen. I listen to the sounds around me, and I listen to my thoughts, realizing that they are only thoughts. When I find myself following a train of thoughts, I gently return my attention to just listening. If I hear the voice of my inner critic, I love it and accept it without believing it, just as I would love and accept a baby who is demanding more ice cream, without my giving him more ice cream.

I cannot change something of which I am unaware, so that awareness is necessary to effect change. Surprisingly, I have often found awareness to be sufficient. With awareness and intent, change frequently happens gradually and effortlessly. Change comes from perceiving and accepting, not from avoiding and rejecting. The renowned humanistic psychologist Carl Rogers (1961, p.17) said, "The curious paradox is that when I accept myself just as I am, then I change.... We cannot change, we cannot move away from what we are, until we thoroughly *accept* what we are. Then change seems to come about almost unnoticed." [italics his]

Think about some aspect of yourself that you reject—some part of yourself you think you need to change. Can you learn to love that aspect of yourself? If I can do it, you can do it. Can you discover a sense of spaciousness in your life in which you are not always controlled by your inner critic, and out of which change happens naturally? You can learn to love and accept yourself exactly as you are. Will it be easy? I do not know. Can you do it? Absolutely.

CHAPTER 5

Seeking

Why do most seekers not become finders? Why do people seeking happiness rarely find joy, satisfaction, and peace of mind? In this chapter, I will present both the obvious and the more subtle problems, perils, and pitfalls which keep them from learning happiness.

Learning a new skill requires practice. And continuing to practice requires discipline, determination, and dedication. In learning to drive a car, maintaining the necessary discipline is easy because the goal is clear and immediate. Learning to play the piano, like learning to be happy, requires more discipline and persistence. I might very well have dropped out of my monthly weekend happiness classes (described in Chapter 6) had it not been for two factors—one planned and one fortuitous—which kept me from quitting.

Far in advance of each month's class, I bought a non-refundable airline ticket. So any last-minute thought of being too busy or too tired to go to class was trumped by the unpleasant prospect of losing money on my airline ticket. I thus set up a situation similar to ones described previously where unexpected growth derived from a dilemma of having to choose the less unpleasant of two events. (The first previous occasion was choosing to strip in the presence of a room full of strangers, rather than publicly refusing to do so. The second occasion was facing my fears and flying solo back to my home airport, rather than facing the embarrassment of telephoning someone to come and get me.) Unlike the previous dilemmas, this one was planned. Had I missed one class, it would have been easy to miss a second, and eventually drop out.

The second factor helping me continue was fortuitous. After the first year, our class was merged with a class which had begun two years previously. So I had the opportunity to observe the results of this teaching through these advanced students. I could not only observe them in class, but I could be with them before and after class, and at meal breaks. They seemed happier than most people and they attributed their happiness to this class. They gave me hope for a similar outcome.

While seeking the serenity, satisfaction, and peace of mind of everyday happiness, we may find it challenging to avoid tempting distractions and diversions. One temptation which can take us off course is the temporary pleasure of acquisitions, such as money and material possessions. Even knowing that such things will not bring us permanent happiness, we may find their lure irresistible. Another temptation is to succumb to the addictive pull of the love, approval, and acceptance of others. Until we have learned to love and accept ourselves exactly as we are, we will continue to seek love, approval, and acceptance from others. But no matter how much love, approval, and acceptance we receive, it will never be enough, especially if we believe ourselves unworthy of it. The strong pull of our culture toward seeking happiness through acquisitions and through attaining approval and admiration is a very strong impediment to becoming a finder. No wonder so many remain seekers.

Impatience is another obstacle in the path toward everyday happiness. It takes time to learn to drive a car, even longer to play the piano, and even longer to attain everyday happiness. One reason that learning to be happy takes so long is the need to unlearn many habitual ways of thinking and being which we have practiced since childhood. We have learned many false beliefs about ourselves which must be unlearned. For example, we may have learned that we are unlovable as we are, and must therefore pretend to be who we are not. We have learned that we should be different, perhaps that there is something wrong with us, or that we have done it wrong and have to do it right. Some people even believe that they don't deserve to be happy.

We have learned to crave money, power, and prestige. We have learned to carefully ration the love we express towards others and especially to ourselves. Unlearning these habitual ways of thinking and behaving takes time and effort. When we don't see immediate results of our efforts, maintaining motivation may be problematic. In the next chapter I will show you a simple technique to experience a small but perceptible increase in happiness in only a few weeks.

Another pothole in the road toward happiness is victimization: the notion that our emotional responses are the results of what others do and say. Rather than take responsibility for how we feel, our culture teaches us to blame circumstances and other people. I recall as a child when clients would frequently telephone my father at home for something trivial. My father would respond angrily, "He gets me so steamed." Similar phrases, such as "You make me happy" or "He has hurt my feelings," are so pervasive in our culture that nobody even considers the possibility that they are blatantly absurd. As I became more aware of my thoughts and emotions, I discovered ever more subtle ways that I had considered myself a victim. As I progressed further on the road to everyday happiness, I was astounded to learn the extent of my personal power—my ability to take responsibility for my thoughts and emotions.

A serious peril causing people to be perpetual seekers is self-help books. I have tried to find happiness through self-help books, but have found them to be of little value. Self-help books and diet books are among the top best-selling works of nonfiction. They also have in common the fact that they usually don't work. Only when I abandoned self-help books and seriously pursued my path experientially by taking action did real progress begin. Self-help books, in telling us how to change, tempt us with a fictional supposedly-better future, while alienating us from the reality of the present moment. Also, those who view the world non-dualistically might claim that self-help books are counterproductive because they foster the illusion of a separate self

Some self-help books are oriented toward changing our external circumstances, such as making friends or accomplishing goals. Even if we succeed in making the desired change, we are inevitably disappointed to find ourselves no happier than before. Other self-help books are oriented toward self-improvement. Because being happy requires abandoning the habitual desire to change ourselves, these books are often counterproductive. They often subtly pander to our inner critic—our voice of self-judgment—thus strengthening it. It is very difficult to make significant change by trying to please our inner critic which tells us we are not acceptable the way we are. For many decades, I read self-help books looking to improve myself and to fix what was wrong with me. But I was on a path which could not possibly succeed, because the inner critic is relentless and never satisfied. It is constantly raising the bar and demanding more. I could never improve enough to satisfy it.

Then, at some point in my reading, I finally discovered that the problem was my inner critic. I thought that what I needed to do to fix myself and be happy was to silence my inner critic. I failed to realize, however, that I was digging myself deeper in a hole by using my inner critic to judge and reject my inner critic. I was still trying to improve myself, and implicitly rejecting myself as I was. Even if I had had this realization, it would have been useless because I would then have used my inner critic to judge and condemn myself for judging and rejecting my inner critic!

Suppose I had read a self-help book containing the previous paragraph, so that I fully realized the depth of the problem. Would that realization have helped? I do not think so because I would have seen the problem, but still not had a solution. No self-help book will teach us how to be happy. We cannot learn how to be happy by reading books and acquiring more knowledge, just as we cannot learn to drive a car or play the piano from reading books.

On the other hand, some books can provide motivation and serve as helpful guides. Books which I have found useful include books by Adyashanti (2006), De Mello (1992), Katie & Katz (2005), Katie & Mitchell (2003), Ruiz (1997), Ruiz (2004), Ruiz & Ruiz (2010), and Tolle (2005). But I warn you again: Reading books can be a vicious trap. Don't be a well-read seeker, when you can be a finder.

Before addressing what has worked to bring me great happiness, I want to mention positive thinking and affirmations, which are commonly used to try to become happy. They may work for some people, but for me they were as counterproductive as self-help books. The idea behind affirmations is to replace "negative" thoughts with "positive" ones, but when repeating an affirmation with which I disagreed, I would feel resistance and disbelief. An affirmation I tried many years ago was "I am beautiful, capable, and lovable." Nice try, but I wasn't convinced! In fact, this affirmation just reinforced my inner critic's view of my insufficiency. Not only did I not feel beautiful, capable, and lovable, but I then had to contend with the feelings of failure I experienced when the affirmation didn't work. For some people an affirmation like, "I pay my bills with love as abundance flows freely through me" might only serve to remind them of how broke they are. These days, my attention is not on thinking positively, but on perceiving reality as it is.

Piling layers of affirmations on top of what is bothering you masks the underlying thoughts which cause your unhappiness, like applying a band-aid to an infected wound. For example, suppose you believe yourself to be unworthy of love. Rather than affirming how lovable you are, I found it more useful to examine the infected belief, "I am unworthy of love." Discover that it is untrue and is causing much grief. In the next chapter, I discuss specific techniques I learned to examine and doubt such stressful thoughts.

Not only does our mind cling obstinately to its beliefs, but a part of our mind sometimes acts as a saboteur. For example, Barbara, the teacher with whom I studied one weekend each month for five years,

65

frequently assigned homework. One assignment was to meditate 20 minutes each day. It was an easy, pleasant assignment, which I fully intended to do. But when I returned to class the next month, I had to report that I had not meditated even once. I felt like a failure, feeling inferior, incompetent, and inept. My teacher then wisely recommended that I only do 5 minutes each day. I returned the following month and reported that I had fully intended to do it, but failed again. At that point, she said lovingly, "Your new assignment, George, is specifically not to meditate. Don't do it!" As you might have guessed, I did exactly the opposite. I felt determined to prove to myself that I had the willpower to meditate. No matter what shape the assignment took, each month I managed to feel justified in berating myself roundly. I can reflect upon this story with humor these days, but it was quite painful at the time.

Many seekers, having read self-help books and learned all about the power of beliefs, do not know that their saboteur, a powerful force, is thwarting any meaningful change. From the previous example, I learned not to underestimate the power of the saboteur.

Don't declare war against your saboteur. Don't do it for two reasons. First, in such a war there are no winners, only losers. The inner conflict will zap your energy, leaving you depleted, discouraged, and distraught. Second, the part of your mind which you identify as "you" will not win. The saboteur is smarter, subtler, and stronger than "you." It is a formidable force which will not be overcome. The saboteur is not malevolent. It was trained at an early age to protect you, and it frequently perceives change as a threat. Rather than confronting and opposing the saboteur, which can be surprisingly clever and cunning, you can learn to accept it. Only then can you hope to befriend it and convert it to an ally.

Barbara claimed that a part of our mind not only sabotages our happiness, but also actively seeks suffering by craving certain familiar, painful emotions. I found this notion hard to accept at first because I believed that we always pursued happiness, although unskillfully. The idea that part of our mind seeks suffering was very alien to me. Then, I was able to notice this urge to suffer in other people, particularly in my wife Carol, as she is closest to me. Only within the past year, have I been able to detect this tendency in myself. Now, I am becoming very aware of how a part of me seeks to suffer. The clearest example was my consistent habit of promising myself to do some task, such as cleaning my study, then not doing it. I then felt guilt and remorse, believing myself to be incompetent and out of control. Then I would repeat my promise to do the task, still not do it, and again feel guilty about it.

My mind also seeks suffering through my habit of rarely completing a job. For example, after doing a simple household repair, I leave a tool out, sometimes for days. Each time I see it, I feel the distress associated with the thought that I should put it away. If I am sufficiently aware, the unpleasant emotion becomes a wake-up call. I can then see the hilarity of leaving one tool out in order to feel bad. It really is funny! And these days I know the way out of this mess is to accept and love myself as I am, rather than listening to my self-judgments and trying to change into a "better" person.

How would you learn to drive a car? How would you learn to play the guitar? In either case, you would find a teacher. For most people, there is no other way. Although becoming a skilled guitarist requires a teacher, you can learn to pick out some chords by yourself. Then, after acquiring this skill, you can choose whether or not to find a teacher.

Is there an analogous practice for happiness— something you can do yourself to become a bit happier? Fortunately, there is. The practice I am about to describe actually does work. I have taught it to others, and it has worked for them. I have since read that some academic psychologists have validated this technique experimentally.

Here's the technique: I find something in my life for which I am truly grateful and then I feel and express that gratitude. That's all. By focusing my attention, I become aware of circumstances for which I am thankful and create the experience of gratitude as a conscious act of will. At first, I was dubious that such a simple technique could have such power, but I can now appreciate the miraculous effect this practice has had on my life.

The most important rule in putting this technique into practice is that the gratitude be real and sincere. Being grateful for something because I think I should doesn't work. By paying close attention, I can be honestly grateful for many seemingly trivial daily situations I might otherwise overlook. I am grateful that my backache is gone. I am grateful that the air-conditioning works in the summer and the heating in the winter. When rolling through a "stop" sign, I am grateful that no police officer is present. I don't try to convince myself that I am grateful. I simply identify those aspects of reality for which I am truly grateful.

There are some instances where I continually experience gratitude. Being pain-free is one. For several, years until it was surgically corrected, I had spinal stenosis, which caused my legs to go numb whenever I stood erect for more than a few minutes. More recently, I've had several bouts of sciatica. As a result, it is very easy for me every day to feel gratitude for the ability to walk normally without pain. For five years, I traveled one weekend each month to a class on how to create a happier life. When I arrived at the airport on the way home, I made a habit of feeling gratitude to find my car intact with no flat tires and no vandalism. Now, it is almost comical: I always feel gratitude when I find my car safe and sound, even after having left it for only a few hours.

I don't mean to imply that I only express gratitude for mundane circumstances. At seventy years old, I am truly grateful that I have eyes that see, ears that hear, and other anatomical parts which function to give me pleasure. I am truly grateful for having enough food, given the number of people in the world who don't. I am truly grateful for having access to decent medical care and clean water, for the loving people in my life, for the gift of good health, and for the fun and excitement of just being alive.

When I first learned of this technique, I made it an intellectual challenge to list items for which I could be grateful. But I missed the point, which is to stop and feel the emotion of gratitude—to experience real appreciation. I was fortunate to have a teacher who guided me in transforming this technique from an intellectual game to a real, felt experience. If you want to be happier, I suggest that you stop reading now and list a few items for which you are grateful. Then review your list, selecting only those for which you can truly experience the emotion of gratitude.

My teachers have told me over and over again, "Practice makes the master." It is certainly true for expressing gratitude. After doing so consciously and willfully, I have found myself doing it habitually. The more I do it, the easier it becomes. For example, my wife Carol is an excellent cook. We don't eat breakfasts or lunches together, but she cooks dinners, and they are delicious and healthful. I don't know whether they are gourmet or not, but I know that I relish them. When I began practicing gratitude, I decided to tell her how much I appreciated her dinners. Now I do it almost every day. But here's the fascinating part of this story: even though my expression of gratitude is habitual, it is not mechanical. I really feel grateful for her wonderful meals, and she enjoys hearing my praise and appreciation.

If you want to make gratitude a permanent part of your life as I have, start noticing ten different items every day for which you are grateful. These items can be small ones: your car started in the morning; despite a massive traffic jam you arrived on time; you found a parking space; your bellyache is gone; you got to the bathroom on time; the sit-com you are watching on television is really funny; you found your keys; your spouse kept his promise; that person looks attractive; this meal is delicious. If convenient, write them down. Spread your observations throughout the day. Get into the habit of noticing all the positive and supportive aspects of your life, and experience the joy of gratitude.

Expressing and feeling gratitude is simple, but it is not always easy. You may find that your mind resists at first. Mine certainly did. The mind is programmed for survival. If our ancient ancestors in Africa had stopped to admire the sunset and to express gratitude for the joys of living, they might have become dinner for the lion which had been stalking them. A function of the mind is to focus attention on possible problems and dangers, but expressing gratitude has little survival value. By consciously paying attention to items for which we are grateful, we can gradually redirect our thoughts away from perceived difficulties and adversities towards practical, everyday reasons for happiness.

In my experience, it is important not to let the gratitude project become a vehicle for self-punishment. If you are as addicted to judging yourself harshly as I was, it is easy for the saboteur to subvert something designed to give pleasure into a way to feel bad. Some books advise keeping a gratitude journal; I don't. The first time you forget to write in your journal, your inner critic will pounce and label you a failure.

Habits can be hard to make and hard to break, and change is difficult to force. So if you find the gratitude project hard to do, cut back. If that doesn't work, just don't do it. Suppose you decide to feel gratitude ten times each day. What happens if one day you forget? What will you do when you are ill or upset and you really don't feel like expressing gratitude? Be gentle with yourself. Expect some bumps and obstacles along the way, and don't judge yourself. What do you do if you find yourself judging yourself? Accept that you are judging yourself and don't condemn yourself for it. If you can, welcome the judgmental way you are. I found it useful to listen to my mind's objections—listen, but not believe. Of course, if you do forget to be grateful and later remember that you should have been, you can always be grateful for remembering.

Why is gratitude so important? It is the quickest route to happiness I have found. Pausing to appreciate the good things in life eradicates troubling concerns without even trying. If I sometimes find myself worrying about the future or regretting the past, I can feel and express gratitude. I quickly disabuse myself of these troubling thoughts and return to joyful equanimity. Any expression of gratitude breaks the momentary spell of fear, judgment, and worry.

CHAPTER 6

Teachers and Transformation

You can become happier by simply practicing gratitude. But for most people, the love and guidance of a teacher are essential to learn true, abiding happiness. Why is this true? How can you find an appropriate teacher? How do you interact most effectively with a teacher? When might it be useful to leave one teacher and find another? My answers to these questions are based on my decades-long experience, including many conversations with teachers and other students. After answering these questions, I will then describe how my teachers have guided me to my transformation and the discovery of my inner truth.

Why a teacher is useful in learning to be happy

A teacher can inspire us, model those qualities we are seeking, provide an aware and supportive environment, assist our practice, and alert us when we veer off course. Slipping is almost inevitable on occasion because learning to be happy requires changing many habitual ways of thinking that have been ingrained for so long that we cannot conceive of alternatives. We may habitually defend our point of view, seeing ourselves as right and others as wrong; we may habitually criticize ourselves and others; we may habitually operate from a sense of fear in order to protect ourselves from potential problems, rather than loving and enjoying life. We learned these ways of thinking when we were young children. For most people, breaking old habits is far harder than forming new ones.

A teacher can help divest ourselves of many false ideas preventing us from enjoying the present moment. A teacher can show us how much we have unwittingly invested in certain core beliefs about ourselves, such as "I am unlovable," "There's something wrong with me," "I don't belong," "I must pretend in order to get love and approval," "I am better than they are." These beliefs are very difficult to dislodge. A part of our mind, which some people call "ego," clings to them tenaciously. A teacher's guidance can help us identify our own versions of such beliefs, so that we can disengage from them.

Most importantly, a teacher can help us recognize our saboteur. It is easy to recognize the saboteur in other people, much more difficult to recognize it in ourselves. In Chapter 5, I described how my saboteur thwarted my efforts to do a simple exercise—meditate 20 minutes a day—causing me undue frustration and disappointment. After acknowledging the saboteur, we can convert it to an ally. I doubt that we can do this without the guidance of a teacher.

For all these reasons, a teacher with whom you have a personal relationship is very useful in learning to be happy. What better way to learn unconditional love for yourself than being in the presence of someone who loves you unconditionally?

Society supports learning to drive. It does not support learning to be happy. Fairy tales, telling us that good people live happily ever after while bad people suffer, further the belief that happiness is the reward for a righteous life. Other people might believe, for example, that happiness results from getting power, money, and sex. In any case, our culture does not support the view that happiness is a learned skill available to everyone. Since the beliefs of people around us strongly influence us, the presence of a teacher and other students can help us maintain our path toward happiness in the face of these cultural biases.

How to find and evaluate a prospective teacher.

My website, www.happinessteachers.com, lists some teachers I can personally recommend. You can also find teachers through a web search, by exploring blogs or social networking sites, or through friends or books.

To learn to play the violin, you would choose a teacher who had mastered the violin, not someone who had written books about it or even acquired a Ph. D. in musicology. Likewise, it makes sense to choose a happiness teacher who has actually learned to be happy. I do not recommend choosing someone who has found happiness from a fortuitous instant transformation. Someone who has successfully gone through the same experience you are embarking on—learning and practicing the skill of happiness—would, in my opinion, be a more effective teacher.

Choose a teacher with whom you feel affinity and rapport—someone whose mode of communication works for you. I know several teachers who teach similar material. I can relate comfortably to some of these teachers, while others appear more remote. Other students appear to connect with teachers whom I have difficulty understanding. As if you were seeking a violin teacher, inquire into your prospective teacher's success in teaching other people to be happy. Speak with current or past students.

I also recommend finding a teacher who does not claim to be special or superior to you. Although some traditions promote revering and paying homage to the teacher, this practice is inconsistent with my experience of happiness as an ordinary skill which anyone can learn. I would respect my violin teacher, but not worship her. Many so-called teachers who require such veneration appear to do so from a need for adulation from others. This need automatically eliminates them as effective happiness teachers.

Avoid teachers who present their path as being the only one, or who insist that their students adopt their beliefs and reject all others. Remember the Chinese expression, "There are many paths to the top of the mountain, but the view is always the same." Choose a teacher who encourages you to explore other possible paths. Skilled teachers, rather than convincing you of the validity of their point of view, will guide you to discover your own truth. A teacher who is judgmental about other people or who tries to distance you from life is still entrapped in ideas of superiority and inferiority and is not ready to teach happiness.

How to interact with a teacher.

To master a particular passage on the violin, you might listen while your teacher plays it, feeling the music and paying attention with all your senses. Learning happiness involves much of the same kind of practice—watching your teacher, listening, and paying attention. Much learning occurs by simply being alert in your teacher's presence. Some people explain this phenomenon as a transfer of "energy" from teacher to student. I see it as an activation of mirror neurons, located in the part of the brain responsible for imitation, learning, and empathy. (These same neurons have us unconsciously mimic each other, for example yawning after someone else yawns.) But, whatever the explanation, be as close to your teacher as possible; if in a class or seminar, sit in the first row; if your teacher allows questions and you have one, ask it. Maximize the time you spend with your teacher.

Most importantly, be open with your teacher. Do not try to please your teacher by pretending to be someone you are not. We have learned as children to pretend in order to get love, appreciation, and approval. Here is an opportunity to experience that you are lovable exactly as you are, with all your supposed faults. Come completely unarmed and authentic. Be willing to be emotionally exposed. And love and accept yourself when you are unwilling to be unarmed, authentic, and emotionally exposed.

Whether to leave a teacher and seek another.

Your emotions may not be a reliable guide to determine whether it is best to leave your teacher. If your chosen teacher does not meet your expectations, you might feel disappointed. When your teacher challenges a core belief, causing you to experience anger or fear, you might want to leave. Such strong emotions can precede a major breakthrough, for every transformation is a "death." Because it is often difficult to distinguish between these very different reasons for wanting to leave, I recommend that you not leave a teacher when you are angry or upset.

Speak with your teacher frankly before taking action. When you are angry or upset—feeling that the teacher has not meet your expectations—you may least want to communicate openly and honestly. But it is essential that you do so.

With patience, you will discover whether it is time to find another teacher, or whether staying and working with your present teacher will prove more fruitful. If you do decide to leave after this period of reflection, you can feel grateful for the experience, forgive yourself and your teacher for any perceived ill treatment, and move on in a healthy way.

My experience with teachers.

These suggestions come from my experiences with a number of teachers, who gave me something valuable and enriched my life. I began by wanting to study with Ken Keyes, Jr. Unfortunately, the only way to study with him was to live full-time in a large residential center he had established, so I never studied with him personally. But each year during Christmas week, he would lead an experiential seven-day program. In Chapter 4, I describe an exercise I did during one such program.

I derived some of my criteria for evaluating a teacher from the negative experience I had with a teacher who had been highly recommended to me. This teacher was intelligent, articulate, cogent, and charismatic. He promised to teach us a new way of being which only he embodied. He claimed we would become more productive and happy. My notes for the first day of class state that he "promises happiness all the time, but we must be sincere with him." He required us to write detailed intimate letters to him. I later discovered that he used these letters from his female students to seduce them. Also, he himself was not happy, and he did not practice the way of being that he professed.

In 2002, my next attempt to find a teacher was more successful. My second teacher, Susan, was the author of a book (Gregg, 2000) I was reading about happiness and transformation. Susan had studied with Don Miguel Ruiz, who had written a best-selling book (Ruiz, 1997) three years previously. Don Miguel is a spiritual guide in the Eagle Knight lineage of the Toltec tradition. His purpose is to teach the ancient wisdom of his ancestors while removing the superstition. In contrast to some previous Toltec teachers, he discourages the use of psychedelic drugs, and he has become well known and highly respected.

I began participating in Susan's weekly group telephone classes. I did not meet her until several months later when she led a trip to Joshua Tree National Park. I later did a retreat with her and fifteen other students in Puerto Morelos, a small fishing village near Cancún, Mexico. During that retreat, I briefly re-experienced the happiness, joy, serenity, and peace of mind that I had last experienced at *est* twenty-five years earlier. While we were playing, throwing each other into a *cenote*,[5] I lost all sense of self-consciousness. I forgot that I wasn't good enough—that I didn't belong. I forgot that I needed to be smarter

---

[5] A *cenote* is a sinkhole containing groundwater, typically found in the Yucatán Peninsula and some nearby Caribbean islands.

than they are. I felt hopeful that I could learn to be happy.

Then, in the spring of 2003, I attended a weekend workshop near my home led by Gary, a teacher who had recently studied with Don Miguel Ruiz. Gary was equally as loving as Susan, but because of his training as an engineer, his communication seemed more logical, linear, and lucid. After that workshop, I concluded that Gary would be a more effective teacher for me. When I telephoned Gary a few weeks later asking to study with him, he wisely set several conditions, one of which required that I clear up any issues I had had with Susan. I was glad to report that I had no issues with her. I studied successfully with Gary for several years by means of two telephone calls per month. In addition, I went on several trips with him and his other students. Gary taught me to listen more carefully to my thoughts and to begin unraveling belief systems by becoming aware of their structure. Most importantly, he taught me the invaluable skill of feeling and expressing gratitude.

While studying with Gary, I participated in several events attended by Don Miguel. At one such event, we were at lunch when someone called out, "Hey Miguel," at the same time tossing a grape in the air in Don Miguel's direction. Don Miguel caught the grape in his mouth, thus completely blowing my image of a guru and best-selling author as someone who is aloof, distant, and reserved. Here was an ordinary, fun-loving guy! I have since spoken with him several times, never having the sense that he thought himself in any way superior to me. Referring to learning to be happy, Don Miguel often said, "If I can do it, you can do it." Another of his famous sayings is "Don't believe me, don't believe them, and especially don't believe yourself."

In the fall of 2004, I attended a three-day workshop led by Don Miguel and another of his students, Barbara. Don Miguel had been leading an intensive course, which met one weekend each month. Because of his recent near-fatal heart attack, Barbara had taken over much of the teaching. I learned that a new class was to begin soon. Both Miguel and Barbara spoke and exhibited such passion and love that I knew in my heart that I had found my path. There was no doubt. I only had one life and if I really wanted to be happy, here was my chance to participate in something more intensive than twice-monthly telephone calls. So I registered for the class.

Before the first weekend, Barbara told us to bring an air mattress or sleeping bag and also appropriate sleepwear for sleeping together in one large room. She required that we continue with our current teacher even after the course began, so I continued my telephone calls with Gary for two more years.

I did not know what to expect as I arrived in Las Vegas for our first class on a Friday evening in April 2005. We initially met in the sanctuary of a former church. At that time, I still considered myself a social misfit, and felt uncomfortable among so many people. Surprisingly, sleeping in a room full of strangers was not a problem (except for some snoring). I was uncomfortable at meal breaks. I dreaded going alone, fearing that my classmates might discover that I did not belong. I felt uncomfortable inviting others to join me in my rental car, and equally uncomfortable waiting for someone to invite me. But these problems gradually resolved as I began to know my fellow students.

Our classes usually had the same format. Most of the time, Barbara would sit on a couch on the dais and speak to us using a microphone. Sometimes, an advanced student would address us, and sometimes Miguel would come. Most students were very excited by Miguel's presence, but I preferred Barbara. I could more easily relate to her way of speaking. She seemed to have an amazing ability to find the perfect word to express what she wanted to convey. When a student asked a question, Barbara would either just answer it or invite the student to join her on the couch for a conversation using two microphones. Occasionally, Barbara would just select a student to invite to the couch. I was chosen often, perhaps because I sat in the front row. Fortunately, I had no difficulty speaking in front of the class because of my training in acting school, experience as an *est* seminar leader, and participation in Toastmasters. I often interjected humor into the conversation, perhaps as a way to impress Barbara and my fellow students.

Miguel and Barbara promised that what we learned would all be common sense. Rather than teach new concepts in which to believe, they would alert us to certain truths that, once presented, were obvious.

For example, they pointed out that we perceive the world through our senses, mostly vision and hearing, but we filter this sensory input through a system of beliefs, expectations, thoughts, and points of view, and we react emotionally to this filtered input. They called that filtered perception "dreaming." Two people can have wildly different emotional reactions to the same event because they construct different dreams.

A basic premise of the course was that we are dreaming all the time. Of course, our daytime dreaming is distinct from our nighttime dreams. At night, we lack most sensory input, so that our dreams are not constrained by reality. I had read books on enlightenment exhorting us to awaken from the dream, but giving little direction on how to do it. This class, in contrast, presented practical tools to create a happier, more loving, and more fulfilling dream.

During the first two years of the class, I complained that I was not any happier. Some of my classmates disagreed, having observed significant positive changes in me. Naturally, I discounted their observations. I saw myself as an introverted, social misfit who was merely becoming more comfortable as he became to know his classmates better.

In 2006, while still studying with Barbara, I read a book by Katie and Mitchell (2003) describing "the Work," a technique specifically designed to help people question their stressful thoughts. This technique seemed in harmony with what I had been learning. Although Barbara and Miguel had taught me the importance of not believing my thoughts, Byron Katie had developed a method of inquiry to accomplish that goal, and I decided to pursue the Work further. Although the Work can be done alone, it is most effective when performed by two people, so I joined a local support group where people met one evening each month to do the Work, and I also did the Work by telephone.

The Work begins with one partner, the client, isolating a particular thought that causes stress. Then the other, the facilitator, guides the client in examining this thought based on four questions: "Is it true?" "Can you absolutely know that it's true?" "How do you react—what happens—when you believe that thought?" "Who would you be without the thought?" After answering these questions, the client suggests various "turnarounds" of the thought and gives three specific instances where each turnaround is as true as, or truer than, the original thought. A turnaround can be a negation of the thought or a variation by changing the subject or object. For example, with the thought "John lies to me," the client can give specific instances of where John is truthful to her, where she lies to John, and where she lies to herself.

Feeling I was pursuing something valuable, in the spring of 2007 I enrolled in a nine-day residential "School for the Work," led by Byron Katie in a hotel in Los Angeles. In some respects, this School was similar to the *est* training: a large number of people meeting for long hours in a hotel ballroom, many unpaid assistants, specific rules, and many surprising experiential exercises. (Divulging these exercises might

85

diminish their impact on future participants, so I will not do so.) During the entire nine-day period, we were instructed not to use makeup, alcohol, drugs, tobacco, or caffeine; not to communicate with home or work except in emergencies; not to read; not to listen to the radio or watch television; and not to eat any food except what was served to the group at mealtime.

The atmosphere at the School was warm and nurturing. Some activities occurred outdoors, either on short walks, in nearby parks, or on field trips. Also, participating in any exercise was optional. If a student asked whether participation was required, the answer was always the same: "This is your school," implying freedom not to participate, but perhaps not deriving the benefit. I chose not to participate in two of the exercises, one involving money, and one involving food. I noticed strong beliefs I had in each of these areas.

I used the Work as a supplement to my studies with Barbara. For the next several years, I did the Work by telephone from three to five days per week with a different partner each month. The person acting as client would choose a stressful thought and the person acting as facilitator would lead an inquiry based on the four questions. We generally alternated being client and facilitator. Although doing the Work in the role of client did not dislodge any of my core beliefs, it was effective on minor annoyances, such as "That shopkeeper is rude" or "I shouldn't have been late." People I facilitated reported similar results from doing the Work. I also found that facilitating others in exploring their stressful thoughts gave me valuable insights into the workings of their saboteur.

Meanwhile, I continued my monthly weekend classes with Barbara, who taught me awareness and self-love. For over half a century, the belief that I was a misfit had dominated my life. It was hard to maintain that belief in the face of the love and acceptance of someone who knew me well, perhaps better than I knew myself. During the third year, that belief and other supporting beliefs began to lessen their grip on me. I felt less fear and less need to hide. As I became more open with people, I found that they accepted me as I really was, not as I had pretended to be. That discovery led to further cracks in the story I had created about my inferiority. Eventually, the whole pyramid of beliefs collapsed. I saw the absurdity of my faulty, fallacious fabrications.

I began to notice my increased love for others and for myself. My love for Carol intensified. I knew that I had always loved her, but I was now experiencing that love as a palpable, joyous sensation I could feel in my body. Situations that used to bother me—like waiting in line, contending with discourteous drivers, or watching the daily news—no longer did. I stopped complaining that I was no happier.

Once each year, instead of the usual weekend class, Barbara's class met for five days in Teotihuacán, a large archaeological site near Mexico City. Some students claimed to feel energy radiating from the pyramids at Teotihuacán; they considered Teotihuacán a holy, spiritual site. I felt nothing special at

Teotihuacán. Having a slight fear of heights, I wished the ceremonies at the top of the pyramids would end, so that I could feel comfortable again on the ground. Nevertheless, the trips to Teotihuacán were trans-formational experiences, affording me opportunities for introspection and seeing areas of my life which were scripted by my beliefs. As I saw how my life had been constricted, constrained, and confined, I opened myself to new experiences—to feel alive, animated, and aware.

In the beginning of my studies with Barbara, I took notes averaging about 2700 words per class. By the last year, my notes had dwindled to about 900 words per class. When I missed a class once, I emailed three of my fellow students requesting a copy of their notes, intending to assemble them into a coherent summary of that month's class. Although the notes contained some overlap, I was amazed by how much they differed, almost as if these three students had attended three different classes, confirming my increased awareness that we all "dream" life differently.

Although the format of Barbara's classes evolved over the years, her ready availability has remained the same. During frequent breaks in the class, we have always been free to consult her privately. Another constant is Barbara's generosity. For example, she conducts free weekly conference calls where current and former students are encouraged to raise whatever concerns we have. At the end of each call, she invites us to telephone her individually, should we feel the need.

Behind all this is Barbara's obvious, palpable, and unconditional love. It is so much easier to accept ourselves when we are so clearly and fully accepted by someone else.

Homework was assigned at almost every class. Sometimes the assignment was to meditate on a certain subject or simply to be aware of certain thoughts or behaviors. Barbara also assigned many exercises to lead each of us toward loving our own body and respecting its wisdom. She also told us to write an autobiography. She said, "Start writing your autobiography. Include the emotions you felt at that time. There are no rules. Play with it. Be creative. Make it your art. Listen to what you tell about yourself and your life. Hear what you think and try not to judge it. With the autobiography, see the emotions that come up. Remember that it didn't happen the way you remember. Your autobiography is a fairy tale."

Each year, as we grew in awareness, Barbara asked us to rewrite our autobiographies. I sometimes rewrote mine from scratch, and other times just revised a previous version. Once, I wrote it in the third person, describing what happened to George. Rewriting my autobiography in these different ways provided me new perspectives on my past. In Chapter 2, for example, I described how my parents lied to me, claiming I was going to the hospital to visit a cousin, rather than to undergo eye surgery. In the past, I used that story to explain why I mistrust and feel distant from people. I also used it to explain why I was unloved, since my parents put their convenience over my welfare. These interpretations about my past influenced how I created my reality.

Writing and rewriting my autobiography showed me the extent to which my reality was created by my interpretation. Realizing this, I was ready to look at forgiveness. There are three levels of what people call "forgiveness." The first level is to take the moral high ground when telling people who have hurt you that you forgive them. You might feel smug and superior because you are doing them a favor by forgiving them. Of course, this is not really forgiveness.

The second level is to truly forgive people who have hurt you, renouncing all claims to retribution and no longer feeling any animosity toward them. This is what most seekers mean by forgiveness.

But I have learned a third level of forgiveness, which I will illustrate with a story about a young couple, both children of immigrants who spoke no English. This couple married in 1933 in the depth of the Great Depression. After having their first child in 1936, the wife lost her second baby and almost died of pre-eclampsia of pregnancy. They loved children so much that despite their doctor's advice not to attempt another pregnancy, they had a second child in 1940, who was normal and healthy, except for being severely cross-eyed. Several years later, having no health insurance, they made the financial sacrifice of arranging elective surgery for him. Out of their love for him, they wanted to save him from unnecessary anxiety by telling him he was visiting a sick cousin, rather than going for surgery. As you might have guessed, I was that young boy. I had previously told a story of how my parents had deceived me and how I had been damaged by their deception. In truth, my parents' deception did not damage or hurt me; it made me stronger—learning to be skeptical, inquiring, and self-sufficient.

The third level of forgiveness is realizing that there is nothing to forgive because it did not happen as we think. In my opinion, this is the only form of true forgiveness. With sufficient insight and willingness to detach from our point of view, we open ourselves to perceiving reality as it is.

I have found nothing that I cannot forgive. For me, this is true liberation.

CHAPTER 7

Love, Joy, and Gratitude

I will devote this last chapter to telling you how I experience life now.

Recently, I noticed a lump in my neck to the right of my windpipe, just above my collar bone. When my doctor advised me to go immediately to the nearest emergency room, my mind raced through three possibilities. First, although unlikely, I considered that the lump could be an aneurysm of my carotid artery, which might burst before I even arrived at the emergency room. Second, the lump could be cancerous, steering my life in a totally different direction, as the projects I considered important would dwarf in importance to this new medical problem. A third possibility was that the lump was benign. After spending hours in the emergency room and discovering that the mass was probably just a benign cyst, I realized that I had remained calm and peaceful throughout this incident— never distressed, anxious, or worried. I remembered how I used to be a chronic worrier.

In the Introduction I said, I "love the world and all the people in it." Let me explain what I mean. We use the word "love" in so many different senses. We fall in love, we love our children, we love chocolate ice cream, and we make love. I love the world and all the people in it by being present to the beauty and magnificence of it all. Paradoxically, enjoying the beauty and magnificence does not preclude preferring that some things be different. But I have almost no expectations nor need to control or change. The world does not have to look a certain way for me to be happy.

You might ask, "How can you love the world, with all the violence, hatred, crime, hypocrisy, greed, suffering, and starvation?"

I would answer "How can I not?" This answer is not flippant; it just describes my experience, which cannot be other than how it is, and which requires no explanation or justification. My love for the world is an almost indescribable sense of gratitude, fascination, attraction, and appreciation. Like viewing the Grand Canyon at sunrise, I do not take in the scene and then complain that some of the rocks should be different. Instead, I am awed by its grandeur and beauty. I marvel at this planet earth, which supports such a wide diversity of life. Instead of judging, comparing and condemning, and so limiting my experience of life, love liberates me to enjoy life's richness and to give what I can. As Einstein said, "One cannot help but be in awe when he contemplates the mysteries of eternity, of life, of the marvelous structure of reality."

I am not "enlightened." Adyashanti, a respected Buddhist teacher, writes "The aim of my teaching is enlightenment—awakening from the dream state....My speaking is meant to shake you awake, not to tell you how to dream better" (Adyashanti, 2006, p. 1). I do not seek enlightenment. I have learned how to dream better. I rarely feel animosity, anger, or antagonism toward anyone. When I read, for example, that some powerful political person is persecuting his citizenry, I prefer that it be different. I perceive that he, like many of us, is seeking happiness unskillfully by habitually responding to his conditioned thoughts. Sometimes, but not often, I can actually feel compassion for him. But usually, I just experience a calm understanding. I no longer feel any anger or frustration when I read the news, not because I don't care about the suffering of others, but because my response is no longer compulsively overrun by my mind's reactions. I have found that when you're angry or antagonistic, it's very hard to respond effectively; on the other hand, freedom from judgment allows truly effective action.

Admittedly, I don't always experience this love, peace of mind, joy, and serenity. Although I rarely criticize events or other people, I still entertain self-judgments, telling myself that I should be better or different. Sometimes, I have enough awareness to recognize these critical thoughts as just meaningless thoughts, and I quickly dismiss them. Other times, I believe them, feeling guilt or shame or remorse or dissatisfac-tion, only later having the awareness to recognize these thoughts as irrelevant. Still other times, I am completely unaware: I hear my thoughts, totally believe them, and suffer the consequences.

Writing this book, for example, has provided me with ample opportunity to lapse into self-judgment: "This paragraph is hard to write; it should be easy." "Why can't I find the right word here?" "This chapter stinks." But the fact that this book is near completion while I am still happy and joyful is ample evidence that I have not yielded to the temptation of believing these stressful thoughts—except for the few times that I have.

Although I have made great progress toward immunity to emotional pain, I am not yet immune to suffering from physical pain. Some people can be happy even when experiencing physical pain, but I cannot. Intellectually, I can understand how it possible. The suffering is caused not by the pain, but the resistance to the pain. Give up the resistance and the suffering vanishes, although the pain persists. But I have so far found this easier said than done.

Every moment represents a crossroads: I can either enjoy life as it is or get caught up in the many fictions manufactured by my mind that take me away from the beauty of the present moment. For example, I fre-quently have the thought, "I can't find my glasses." This is not merely a statement of fact. I recognize it as a self-judgment because of my emotional responses—guilt, irritation, and discouragement— which manifest as tightness in my solar plexus, tension in my jaw, and a general feeling of discomfort. I also notice underlying thoughts like "I should be able to find them" and "I should have put them away."

On further examination, there are three fascinating aspects of this thought. The first is its frequency: I probably think this thought, with its accompanying unpleasant emotional responses, three or four times each week. The second is its history: I can almost hear my mother telling me as a young child, "If you'd put things away, you'd know where they are." Whether the item is my glasses, keys, wallet, tools, or pen, I've internalized this criticism since childhood. The third is the ease with which I can entertain further critical thoughts about this self-judgment: Once I get started along the road of self-blame, my mind seems willing to pile on more blame in whatever fashion it can devise. For example, I can easily lapse into thoughts like, "George, you are a fraud. You claim you've learned how to be happy, yet you still beat yourself when you can't find something," or "You should have given this up years ago!"

I have found these thoughts easy to counter merely by recognizing the truths: "I am not a fraud just because I still have some remaining self-judgments. It takes time to overcome habitual ways of thinking, and I have only recently gained awareness of these particular thoughts." Indeed, lovingly recognizing them for what they are—reactive thoughts—seems to make them dissolve without effort.

Extricating myself from the underlying thoughts, "I should be able to find them" and "I should have put them away" is more challenging. I have believed these "shoulds" without question for decades and there is an element of truth in them. However, something is radically different now. That difference is the light of awareness which I have shone on these thoughts by writing about them. Now that I hear them consciously and recognize them as mere thoughts, I will respond skeptically and calmly, as I have with other thoughts once I become aware.

I am most happy when I express love. I express love to myself by doing what I enjoy and having fun. I express love to my body by giving it what it wants, such as healthful foods, exercise, water, air, sunlight, sex, and ample rest. I express love to others through kindness, respect, and generosity. I also express love to others by teaching what I have learned. The following is an excerpt of a conversation using text on the internet with a former short-term student whose huband was discouraged because he couldn't find meaningful work.

Me: *When someone we love is unhappy or has a problem, there are only two things to do: First, love that person. Express your love fully. Second, Love yourself. Express your love to yourself.*

Student: *Thank you. I've been doing the first, but not the second. No wonder I've felt depleted.*

Me: *The second is the more important....*

Student: *Yes. Now that you've reminded me, I will.*

Me: *Express your love for yourself. Do it in words, but most importantly do it in action.*

Student: *Yes...I can think of several ways that come immediately to mind.*

Me: *That's perfect.*

Student*: It really is.*

Me: *You will be happier, and he will be happier.*

Student: *And you will have quietly had a wonderful impact on a little part of the world.*

Me: *Thank you, dear. Those words mean a lot to me.*

Student: *I always come away from conversations with you feeling the richer for them.*

I felt great, when I read those last two sentences from my former student. What a wonderful opportunity for me to repay the world the bounty I have received from my own teachers.

Teaching is a valuable experience for me for a number of reasons. When I teach, I am in the present moment. I don't prepare what I am about to say. I hear it as I speak it. It comes from the heart. Also, teaching makes what I have learned more real. I frequently tell my students, "Love yourself **exactly** as you are." If I could, I would proclaim this prescription from a mountain top, shout it from a pulpit, or insert it electronically into the loudspeaker system at a football game. The reason I am so adamant about this one prescription is that it is the one I most need to hear. When I teach, I am my best student.

I believe I have now reached the point that I am immune to most emotional pain, but I cannot know for certain that that is true. Perhaps some future event will trigger suffering. But if that happens, I have many tools to regain my equanimity. First, I can stop and pay attention to my breathing, taking a few slow, deep breaths. Second, I can seek aspects of the event for which I can sincerely feel authentic gratitude. If I cannot do that, I can seek other aspects of my life for which I experience gratitude. Third, I can sit in my meditation chair and allow myself to feel without resistance whatever emotions I am experiencing, such as fear, anger, or sorrow. Toward that end, I might try to locate specific places in my body where I feel those emotions. By doing this, I can identify the thoughts that cause the unwanted emotion—thoughts about the past, such as "This shouldn't have happened," or fearful thoughts projecting an imagined future. Once I become aware of the underlying thoughts, I can begin to question them. I might use the Work, described in Chapter 6, to help me doubt the thought. Rather than doing this myself, I could find someone else experienced in the Work to ask me the four questions and guide me through the turnarounds. Someone not caught up emotionally as I am can frequently guide me to the truth. Lastly, I could telephone my teacher Barbara. A short phone conversation might be all I need to awaken me from the hellish virtual reality caused by the false beliefs which entangle me.

Nine months ago, after having written the previous paragraph, and just when I thought I would "live happily ever after," I was hit by a bout of clinical depression—not just sadness, but full clinical depression, including suicidal thoughts. My doctor diagnosed the depression, explained that clinical depression was caused by a chemical imbalance in the brain, and prescribed an antidepressant.

But the depression continued to worsen. Shortly after waking and while still in bed, I would sometimes feel myself descending into what seemed like a rabbit hole into hell. When Carol responded to my calls for help, I would grab onto her as if she were my only lifeline to reality. I eventually learned to avoid these terrifying incidents. As soon as I felt an impending episode, I would force myself to rise from bed and walk around the house vigorously.

The depression totally distorted and corrupted my normal thought processes. For example, I considered the advantages and disadvantages of various practical methods of killing myself. Fortunately, I never reached the stage of actually attempting any, but I now understand how depressed people can be driven to suicide.

Although it was difficult to feel joy or gratitude while depressed, my having learned to be happy helped me in two important ways. First, I had sufficient love for myself to take forceful steps to hasten my recovery. I consulted a psychiatrist who tripled the dose of antidepressant and arranged for brief weekly follow-up appointments. Second, recalling how happy I had been and longing to be happy again motivated me to take actions which would otherwise have been too difficult. For example, I forced myself to exercise and to eat. I also agreed to accompany Carol while she shopped, even though I would much have preferred to stay home. I spoke with Barbara, who made some useful suggestions. What was most valuable was the love and support I experienced from the people around me, especially Carol and my children.

After four weeks, the depression suddenly lifted. My bout of clinical depression was quite a trip. Looking back at this incident, I find it hard to appreciate that I am the same person who entertained those suicidal thoughts. Depression, I discovered, is very different from sadness. William James (1902; 1999 reprint, p.165) described depression as "a positive and active anguish, a sort of psychical neuralgia wholly unknown to normal life."

Many seekers know that we create our own reality in the sense that we perceive and interpret the world through the filter of our beliefs, thoughts, and expectations. I was flabbergasted to learn that we do not directly perceive reality; instead, our brain uses visual input to construct a *model* of reality based on our beliefs, expectations, and memory. According to David Knill, Professor of Brain and Cognitive Science, "We mistakenly think of human vision like a camera. We have this metaphor of an image being cast on the retina and we tend to think of vision as capturing images and sending them to the brain." (See Hagan, 2012, p. 35)

If you are as incredulous as I was, read the first few chapters of Metzinger (2009), a non-technical, philosophical discussion of perception as a creative process. He states that "Modern neuroscience has demonstrated that the content of our conscious experience is not only an internal construct, but also an extremely selective way of representing information." (p. 6). If you need further convincing, read either of the books by Purves and Lotto (2003, 2010), which, through numerous photos and diagrams, will remove all doubt. A professor at the Harvard Medical School writes, "Perception is a collaboration between representations brought to our brain by our senses and information already coded there in memory" (Hobson, 1999, p. 70). We are not passive observers; the brain uses sensory input to actively create an internal model—a representation of the world—based on recalled information. There is no color green out there, and the falling tree does not make a sound when no brain is present to create it.

Why is it important to appreciate that our perceptions are self-created? Here's why: Just as you cannot know clinical depression without having experienced it, you cannot know the created reality of another human being. Your spouse, lover, boss, parents, and children inhabit totally different worlds from you. Their creations are as valid as yours. Fully appreciating this fact is the cornerstone for respect, compassion, understanding, and love.

My emotional experience of happiness these days, except when I am ill or in pain, mostly varies between two states. In the first state, which I experience most of the time, I am happier than I have ever been. And although I am occasionally annoyed, sometimes fretting or complaining, those breaks from equanimity are short-lived. For the most part, I am content, peaceful, and optimistic, while enjoying life. In the second state, which I experience rarely, perhaps several times a week, I become joyful—almost ecstatic. Nothing fazes me. I have a huge smile on my face. It's like being high on marijuana, except that I can function normally. I will sometimes join Carol while she is watching a situation comedy on TV. The jokes which I normally thought dumb, I now find enormously funny.

I have been blessed with a great toy to play with— a brain consisting of one hundred billion neurons which mysteriously gives rise to consciousness. I can see, hear, taste, feel, smell, talk, think, and laugh. My body has an amazing immune system, and is self-healing; when I cut myself, for example, new skin grows to heal the injury. Now that I'm 70, I don't know how much longer I will get to enjoy this toy—perhaps 20 years, perhaps 10 years, perhaps 42 days. But I intend to enjoy every day until the day I die, at which time I will be grateful for having had the opportunity to play.

When it is time to go, I can only say, "Thank you."

Bibliography

Adyashanti, "Emptiness Dancing," Second Edition, Sounds True, 2006.

Brickman, P., Coates, D., Janoff-Bulman, R., *Lottery winners and accident victims: Is happiness relative?"* Journal of Personality and Social Psychology, Vol. 36(8), Aug, 1978. pp. 917-927.

De Mello, A, "Awareness: The Perils and Opportunities of Reality." Doubleday, 1992.

Fowles, J., "Starstruck: Celebrity Performers and the American Public", Smithsonian Institution Press, 1992.

Gregg, S., "The Toltec Way: A Guide to Personal Transformation," Renaissance Books, 2000.

Hagan, S., *The Mind's Eye* Rochester Review, March-April 2012.

Hobson, J. A., "Dreaming as Delirium: How the Brain Goes Out of Its Mind," MIT Press, 1999.

James, W., "The Varieties of Religious Experience: A Study of Human Nature," (1902). Reprinted as Modern Library paperback, (1999).

Katie, B. & Katz, M., "I Need Your Love--Is That True," Harmony Books, 2005.

Katie, B. & Mitchell, S. "Loving What Is: Four Questions that Can Change Your Life," Three Rivers, 2003.

Keyes, K. Jr., "Handbook to Higher Consciousness" Fifth Ed., Living Love Center, 1975.

Lutter, M., *Book review: "Winning a lottery brings no happiness,"* Journal of Happiness Studies (2007) 8:155-160.

Metzinger, T., "The Ego Tunnel: The Science of the Mind and the Myth of the Self," Basic Books, 2009.

Purves, D. & Lotto, R.B., "Why We See What We Do: An Empirical Theory of Vision," Sinauer Associates, 2003.

Purves, D. & Lotto, R.B., "Why We See What We Do Redux: A Wholly Empirical Theory of Vision," Sinauer Associates, 2010.

Rogers, C., "On Becoming a Person: A Therapist's View of Psychotherapy," London: Constable, 1961.

Ruiz, M., "The Four Agreements: A Practical Guide to Personal Freedom," Amber-Allen, 1997.

Ruiz, M., "The Voice of Knowledge: A Practical Guide to Inner Peace," Amber-Allen, 2004.

Ruiz, M. & Ruiz, J., "The Fifth Agreement: A Practical Guide to Self-Mastery," Amber-Allen, 2010.

Tolle, E., "A New Earth: Awakening to Your Life's Purpose," Dutton/Plume 2005.

25028256R00063

Made in the USA
Lexington, KY
09 August 2013